JB JOSSEY-BASS™
A Wiley Brand

Foundation & Corporate Grants

How to Improve Your Funded Grants Batting Average

Scott C. Stevenson, Editor

WILEY

978-1-118-69199-1   ISBN

978-1-118-70431-8   ISBN (online)

Foundation & Corporate Grants:
How to Improve Your
Funded Grants Batting Average

Published by
Stevenson, Inc.
P.O. Box 4528 • Sioux City, Iowa • 51104
Phone 712.239.3010 • Fax 712.239.2166

www.stevensoninc.com

Foundation & Corporate Grants: How to Improve Your Funded Grants Batting Average

FOUNDATION/CORPORATE RELATIONS BASICS

Whether you're in the beginning stages of seeking foundation and corporate grants or have been at it for a while, this chapter offers some tried-and-tested principles that will help to improve your odds of securing grants and also shares key procedures that will make your grant-seeking efforts run more smoothly and effectively.

In Search of Grants: Grant-seeking Procedures for Beginners

Have you tried to obtain funding through grant proposals, only to turn up empty handed time and again? Or do you simply keep missing grant application deadlines?

Securing foundation funding requires extra effort, but the results can take your organization to the next level. Following these six steps should help you focus your efforts and begin successfully securing grants for your cause:

Research —

The first step is to find foundations that fund your type of organization and project. A number of resources provide information on private, community and corporate foundations, and these often include details on past grant recipients and programs.

Look for funders whose priorities closely match your project, focusing on subject (arts, education, healthcare), type of support (scholarships, building campaigns, operating funds) and geographic areas (national, regional, statewide). Identify foundations that intersect all areas for the project that is under consideration.

Also look at past recipients and grant amounts, which can tell you if they have a history of funding organizations and projects like yours for the amounts you need.

Search through hard-copy or online directories or use electronic or CD-ROM resources to create lists of potential prospects. Check out area libraries and foundation center collections if you don't have the resources in-house.

Request —

Once you have identified your prospects, get a copy of each foundation's guidelines, application forms and annual reports. Their funding priorities may have changed since directories were published, and this is a way to make sure your project fits before you write your proposal. You can call, write or get the information from the foundation's website.

Write —

Although each foundation has specific guidelines and requirements, create an outline for all proposals. The main parts of a proposal include an executive summary; statement of need for project, project description and timeline; budget outline; and general information about your organization. Be concise and persuasive, including only what they request.

Relationships —

As with other types of fundraising, connections and ties can make a big difference in your success. If you have board members or other supporters with connections to the foundation, have them send follow-up letters in support of your proposal.

Contact the foundation during the proposal-writing process. Program officers will often share clues to make your proposal more successful. They will also tell you if your project will more than likely not be funded by them. Both situations can save you a great deal of time. Visit them in person if possible.

Once you get an answer from the foundation, positively or negatively, follow up. If you are not funded, call and ask the program officer how you could change your proposal and when you can resubmit it. If you are funded, thank the foundation in writing and follow through with any project reporting requirements.

Recognition —

In addition to a standard gift acknowledgement, promote the grant to the community and your constituency. Work with the foundation to determine the level of publicity with which its representatives are comfortable. Marketing your success can often leverage additional funding from others. Good stewardship also leads to opportunities for future asks from the same foundation.

Recordkeeping —

Create a system to identify appropriate prospects, keep the process working smoothly, ensure that deadlines are not missed and help develop relationships with funders. This system should streamline your ability to track your prospects, including their interests, deadlines and contact information.

Record the dates, amounts, and projects when you submit proposals.

Set up ticklers to remind you when decisions are due, when to follow up with the foundations, and when reporting requirement dates fall.

Use Common Sense When Submitting Proposals

Here are some tips to make your grant proposals more successful. Although they seem simple and straightforward, they are too often ignored.

1. **Check the contact information.** Make sure you send the proposal to the right address and the appropriate person, especially if the foundation has different program officers for different types of funding.

2. **Ask for a specific amount in your request.** If you don't tell the foundation representatives how much you want from them they won't know.

3. **Ask for the right amount.** Determine the average range of gifts the foundation has made in the past. Research the amounts specific to your type of request.

4. **Make sure your request fits within the foundation's guidelines**, including geographic or funding area restrictions. Don't ask for operating funds for a hospital if all the foundation funds are capital campaigns for higher education.

5. **Show how the foundation's grant will fit into your overall plan.** Are you asking a foundation to pay for the entire project? How will you fund future needs? Do you need their grant to help finish a capital campaign? If you've stated a need or problem, indicate the solution and what part the foundation will play in that solution.

6. **Demonstrate that you have the support of others for your organization, and this project specifically.** Include other foundations, corporations and individuals who have already donated or will be working with you to make it work.

7. **Follow up on your proposal.** If successful, be good stewards and thank them appropriately, including providing any reports or agreements they require in return for the grant. If you are turned down, thank them for having considered your request, then learn how to improve future (perhaps reconsidered) proposals.

Concept Paper Helps Shape Funding Proposals

Before pursuing a grant or gift for a new project, take the time to think it through. Draft a one- or two-page concept paper that addresses these basic questions:

- What will this project accomplish?
- Why is it important to do it?
- How will it be done and by whom?
- How much will it cost?

This initial planning will better prepare you for securing the needed funds.

Practical Advice for Approaching Foundations

As you work to establish and maintain positive relationships with foundation representatives:

1. Understand the foundation's purposes, preferences and pattern of past support. Be sure they are compatible with your charity's priorities.

2. Proposals should connect their mission with yours, along with future plans.

3. If you utilize board members or others in connection with a foundation call, give them a role to play, not simply window dressing.

4. Provide progress reports if a grant is received, whether or not they are requested.

Do You Have an Active Grants Committee?

Successfully managing any committee requires time. But it's a worthwhile investment, as a well-represented, well-managed grants committee can result in big dividends.

To create or improve an existing committee, consider these factors:

✓**Committee composition** — Who should you enlist? If you're fortunate enough to have people with links to foundation or corporate boards, they will make a natural fit. Also, look to your nonprofit's employees, who can help identify and articulate funding opportunities. Don't

exclude individuals from dissimilar nonprofits who have had success at landing grants for their agencies.

✓**Responsibilities** — Likely duties include identifying funding sources; corporate and foundation research; delineating and prioritizing funding opportunities; reviewing and/or refining draft proposals; making corporate and foundation calls, and more.

✓**Operation** — Keep committee size manageable, say five to eight members who meet an hour a month to discuss issues from a prepared agenda distributed in advance.

Prioritize Funding Needs, Amounts

Those persons responsible for developing grant proposals at your institution can benefit from having a one-year (or multi-year) operational plan that not only prioritizes funding needs, but also quantifies deadlines and target amounts.

As you map out quantifiable funding objectives for a year or more, categorize them within the following groups: program goals, equipment goals, project goals and personnel goals. Here is a template to get you started:

		For What	By When	For How Much
Program Goals:	1.			
	2.			
	3.			
Equipment Goals:	1.			
	2.			
	3.			
Project Goals:	1.			
	2.			
	3.			
Personnel Goals:	1.			
	2.			
	3.			

Know What's Important to a Foundation

For many corporations and foundations, selecting grantees is based somewhat on the process of elimination. With so many deserving requests, it becomes necessary to eliminate some, even though they may be well-written and worthy of funding.

Knowing what a foundation looks for can help you understand your organization's strengths and weaknesses and where you may need to make internal improvements.

Here are some common areas of interest that foundations consider as they prioritize possible grant recipients:

✓ **Record of growth, achievement.** What has your non-profit accomplished in fulfilling its mission? How has it distinguished itself from similar organizations?

✓ **Financial strength.** What does your most recent audit reveal? Have you achieved balanced budgets in recent years? Has gift support increased?

✓ **Diversity of funding base.** What are your sources of annual revenue? Who are your primary sources of gift support? Has your donor base broadened over time?

✓ **Cash reserves.** Are you financially prepared for emergencies? Do you have an equipment and/or operations reserve?

✓ **Active board.** Who makes up your board? Are they engaged and committed as both donors and volunteers?

✓ **Staff competency.** What is the quality of your top management? How long have they been with your nonprofit?

✓ **Program delivery.** Do you, in fact, provide the services you purport to provide?

✓ **Shared vision between staff and board.** Does the board support management's long-range plans?

✓ **Cost per unit of service.** What does it cost to provide a particular program? How many will benefit in relation to its cost?

✓ **Duplication of efforts.** Is another agency providing services you hope to provide?

✓ **Comparison to a social cost.** How badly needed is the program in relation to other social services?

✓ **Degree of risk.** Can the project realize its aims if the funding is provided? Will the nonprofit survive the next decade?

Create a Policy for Accepting Corporate, Naming Gifts

When a nonprofit accepts a major naming gift or enters into a marketing co-venture with a company, the name of the nonprofit becomes linked with its partners, and any negative press and impressions of that company will affect the nonprofit, says Theresa Nelson, principal, Theresa Nelson & Associates (Oakland, CA).

Nonprofits should enter into such a partnership only after a rigorous, objective process to create a gift acceptance policy outlining the criteria that must first be met, Nelson says. That criteria should include whether the company is a good fit with the nonprofit's mission; what would be required of your organization; and a risk analysis.

"You need to ask yourselves, 'Will this corporate naming opportunity put us at high risk for negative publicity?'" she says. "Above all, you need to protect your own interests. You need to have an escape clause in case the company brings bad publicity to your organization. When something hurts the identity of your organization, it turns away donors and affects your reputation and ability to raise funds."

Address the issue of major corporate naming before it becomes a reality, says Nelson, because once you have one group excited about a gift, and one group opposed, the question changes from whether you will accept naming gifts from companies at all, to "Do we like this company?" which can become a very heated issue.

Other areas to address in a corporate gift acceptance policy, she says, include:

* Any exceptions, e.g. corporations that you would never take donations from under any circumstances.

* Levels of recognition.

* What permanent naming privileges to offer, or if you should even offer naming opportunities to corporations.

"Organizations can normally easily determine companies they would always take gifts from and those they would never take gifts from," says Nelson, "but it's the ones in the middle that require some thought — and a gift acceptance policy."

Source: Theresa Nelson, Principal, Theresa Nelson & Associates, Oakland, CA. Phone (510) 420-0539. E-mail: nelsontm@pacbell.net

Ways to Seek the Help of a Grant Writer

Many nonprofits aren't large enough to merit hiring a full-time grant writer but know they may be missing out on some foundation, corporate or even government grant opportunities.

If your charity falls into this category here are some ways you might be able to address that issue:

✓ Hire a grant writer whose duties go beyond foundation and corporate grants proposals: preparing proposals for individuals; writing copy for publications; writing speeches; and more.

✓ Collaborate with other non-competing nonprofits in hiring a grant writer who will represent each participating organization on an equal basis.

✓ Consider outsourcing grant writing to a company that specializes in such work (see sampling of companies).

✓ Seek assistance from one of many grant writers' associations (see sampling of associations).

Sampling of Grant Writing Companies, Consultants

GrantLinks.net — http://grantlinks.net

Grant Writer — www.grantwriter.com

Research Associates — www.grantexperts.com

Seliger + Associates — www.seliger.com

Sampling of Grant Writers Associations

American Grant Writers' Association — www.agwa.us

Puget Sound Grantwriters Association — www.grantwriters.org

Proposal Pitfalls to Avoid

As much as you may want or need corporate or foundation funding, don't twist your nonprofit's needs or improperly describe circumstances to meet a prospective funder's expectations. Poorly prepared documents or misstated information will eventually be recognized by foundation representatives and prove detrimental to future funding.

As you craft proposals, follow these guidelines:

1. **Don't miss funding deadlines.** Whether a foundation meets annually, quarterly or monthly, having your proposal arrive post-deadline reflects poorly on your nonprofit.

2. **Don't write a generic proposal that you mail to several foundations.** Corporate and foundation representatives network just like development professionals and can identify proposals that are boilerplate in nature.

3. **Don't overstate your case.** Be honest. Tell it like it is. Just as you shouldn't exaggerate what a grant will do for your organization, neither should you promise more than your nonprofit can deliver if you would, in fact, receive a grant.

4. **Don't bluff.** If you've experienced a budget deficit in recent years, don't try to hide it. Foundations would much rather know the facts than have to read between the lines and question your integrity.

5. **Don't back door a foundation.** Perhaps your co-worker is a cousin to a friend of a foundation trustee's nephew. Forget it. Foundation staff do not appreciate those who try to go around the system to get favorable attention for proposals, nor do foundation trustees appreciate being lobbied for special attention.

High-impact Moves for Securing Grants

As you seek program funds from corporations, don't overlook these key actions:

1. **Get corporate involvement.** Corporations often keep funds close to where employees live. Provide regular corporate volunteer involvement opportunities. Corporate foundations of all sizes give to causes with which employees are involved.

2. **Cultivate personal relationships.** A call to the corporation's community affairs department and follow-up correspondence can break recognition barriers as your proposal is reviewed in the wake of intense competition. Build on that relationship to the greatest extent possible.

3. **Identify projects that capture corporate attention.** Recognize the balance needed between your nonprofit's priorities and what corporations find most self-serving. The benefits they perceive will tilt grant odds in your favor.

When is a Grant Agreement a Contract, Not Just a Gift?

Q. *"If a foundation requires in its grant agreement with an organization that the funds must be returned if the organization does not perform in accordance with the purposes of the approved grant request, does that make the grant a contract and not a philanthropic gift?"*

"By definition a grant is a gift. Grants from organizations such as foundations are usually conditional, but that does not make them automatically contractual. A contract requires consideration (mutuality of obligation) by both parties to each other. The requirement that the intent of the grant be carried out or it be returned is a standard practice by most funding organizations, and is a condition but doesn't automatically mean there is consideration. In addition, if there is donative intent by one of the parties, then there is no consid-

eration and, hence, no contract. Pledges to make gifts can be enforced when there is reliance, but that does not make them contractual. I think an attempt to label the grant as a contract based on this language in the gift agreement is a stretch."

— *Peter M. Wasemiller, Director of University Grants & Research, Fresno Pacific University, (Fresno, CA)*

"Under U.S. tax law, unless a funder receives something of potentially marketable value (e.g., copyright, patent, ownership of research results) in exchange for their money, it's a charitable gift and not a contract/grant. A contract or grant must include an exchange transaction of some kind. If no exchange occurs, it's a gift."

— *Dennis Alexander, Director of Foundation Relations, Texas Christian University (Fort Worth, TX)*

Should You Outsource Grant Writing?

If you don't have funds for an in-house grant writer, look at contracting with one.

"By its nature, grant writing is a time-consuming business made all the more difficult for staff that might be unfamiliar with the process," says Dhyana Kearly, a grant-writing consultant based in Redmond, OR. "An inexperienced grant writer could easily spend two or three times the hours completing a grant application process and find themselves much less successful than someone more familiar with the process and expectations of foundations and grant makers in general."

Kearly answers some questions about hiring a freelance grant writer:

What are the advantages of using a freelance grant writer over an in-house one?

"I would assume that an in-house grant writer would be just as successful as a freelance grant writer when it came to submitting proposals. The key to writing proposals has more to do with having a solid understanding of the organization combined with consistent grant writing experience that can only be achieved over time. One advantage a freelance grant writer might bring to the picture would be his or her experience with a variety of projects, and therefore greater access to a wider range of grant maker's information. The freelance grant writer may also have developed stronger working relationships with state and local funders, which could benefit the applicant organization."

Should you use a freelancer for one-time projects or for ongoing grant projects?

"Freelance grant writers are usually equally available for one-time as well as ongoing projects. However, it behooves an organization to keep on their speed dial for future projects a grant writer with whom they may have already developed a successful funding relationship. One of the key elements in achieving favor from grant makers has to do with a grant writer's familiarity with an organization and his or her ability to eloquently and clearly communicate that organization's mission, projects and goals."

How can you educate a freelance grant writer about your organization so he or she can communicate your mission and needs effectively to a prospective foundation grantor?

"A good grant writer will aggressively work to quickly gain an intimate understanding of an organization's services, projects, program and mission by interviewing staff, board members and even volunteers; by reading all available published materials; by visiting an organization's website; and by doing additional research as needed. Having this sort of data readily available will make the grant writer's job just that much easier."

What should you not expect from a freelance grant writer?

"Do not expect a grant writer to work miracles, although that occasionally does happen. Organizations need to understand that successful funding is better accomplished when staff and board are equally informed and dedicated to the project. It is good to keep in mind that the success of a grant is only partially due to the ability of the grant writer. Having a client to write for that has a history of successful endeavors, a solid board of directors and a reliable body of volunteers, as well as a history of successful management strategies, also helps. A gifted grant writer might be successful in bringing a grant maker to the table to support most any project, but if the people representing the organization are not prepared to demonstrate their own merit, more often than not, funding will be denied."

What is the best way to fund a freelance grant writer?

"Resources need to be readily available to pay for a freelance grant writer in the same way that they are for an organization's other employees, although freelance grant writers will usually supply a contract for services prior to beginning work. Grant-writing professionals with a background in successfully achieving awards mostly feel that it is not only unethical to sign contingency contracts with clients (e.g., writing a grant proposal in anticipation of its being funded), but it is also bad practice. Some funders will refuse to fund projects with grant-writing contract overhead built into them. In addition, working under a contingency contract can be a gamble when dealing with nonprofits that are notorious by nature for routinely changing management staff, administrative personnel and board of directors, any of whom might choose to cancel a contingency contract put in place by their predecessors, which could leave a grant-writing consultant severely in the lurch."

Source: Dhyana Kearly, Grant Writing Consultant, Redmond, OR. Phone (541) 508-0960. E-mail: dhyana@harmoniousway.com

Can You Justify Not Hiring a Grant Writer

Time keeps getting more precious and resources continue to be stretched for nonprofits. Some days it seems like you're wearing so many hats you can't see straight. One of the areas that may suffer because of this situation is getting funding through grant proposals. If you have someone already on staff to handle them, or if you're thinking of adding this method to your fundraising toolbox, the following points can help you keep in mind the importance of a grant writer.

Why Do You Need a Grant Writer?

The forms required as part of a grant proposal are getting more and more complicated to fill out. This means more time and attention must be devoted to them if you are to be successful. That's more time taken away from other forms of solicitation.

Foundations are attaching more requirements to their proposals, such as detailed project budgets, descriptions of how the project will impact the community, and analyses of outcomes. In addition, reporting requirements are often more detailed and more frequent once the grants are awarded. You'll need someone who can stay on top of these so you can continue to go back to the same foundations.

As the number of nonprofit organizations increases and the funding needs of existing groups are harder to meet, the competition for grants continues to grow. It's not enough to have a worthy cause anymore. Now you have to make your case more compelling than all the other worthy causes.

Many foundations are beginning to call for proposals for specific needs they feel should be addressed, instead of providing grants for programs the nonprofits generate on their own. This means you need to keep abreast of what the foundations are doing and new initiatives they are creating so your organization can tap into that funding.

Individuals are creating wealth for themselves at an amazing rate through investments and high-tech companies. As they grow richer, many are putting aside money into their own foundations. Nonprofits must now approach individuals in different ways, and often with more formal grant proposals than previous informal solicitations.

What to Look For in a Grant Writer

Grant writers should have specific skills and talents, and you may not be able to simply hand this task over to someone already on staff.

Proposals are more than merely compiling information, although that is a part of what grant writers need to be able to do. They should also have strong organizational skills and the ability to follow instructions with an eye for detail. Foundations have been known to drop proposals in the first cut just because applicants used the wrong binding on the document or several words were misspelled.

> **Role of Grants Professional**
>
> - **Grantsmanship:** The aim of a successful grants person should be to identify needs of legitimate value to the organization and to match those needs with the interests of foundations and corporations.

As the title suggests, this person needs to be able to write and write well. Proposals need to be persuasive and concise, and the writer needs to be talented enough to make compelling arguments for any type of program or project. Technical knowledge of the program may not be necessary, but the grant writer definitely needs the ability to make the technical details understandable by the grants committees.

How to Accomplish Your Goals

Even if you have no track record of funding from grant proposals, a grant writing position can be justified. It only takes one successful proposal that might not otherwise have been funded to pay for the position. (Like other fundraising positions, however, a grant writer should not be paid on commission as a percentage of successful proposals for a number of reasons.)

If you can't afford a salaried position, there are a number of writers available to work on a contract basis. You could pay per proposal or for a set period of time.

Several nonprofits in an area could pool together to pay for a shared grant writer. Confidentiality agreements and job requirements should be specifically outlined and agreed upon by all parties before hiring anyone for the job.

Nonprofits that don't have the resources or the need for a full-time grant writer could add other responsibilities to the position. Some logical options would be research, direct mail, or other writing duties like newsletters.

What You Should Know About Going After Federal Grants

To secure a federal grant, your institution has to be ready, says Lynne McKenna Frazier, director of corporate and foundation relations, University of St. Francis (Fort Wayne, IN).

"It's a mind-set that's necessary," Frazier says. "There must be real buy-in, including an understanding of the amount of time that's required. It starts with your immediate supervisor, but the academic side in particular has to be ready to make this investment."

She shares additional advice for going after federal grants:

✓ No matter how much time you allow before the deadline, it's not enough. "I spent a year working with one group and will spend a year working with another on a different application," she says. "There's usually only 30 to 60 days between posting and deadline, but many programs are repeated annually, so you can start work that far in advance."

✓ Be prepared for a lot of hand-holding as you go through the process. Keep the guidelines in front of everyone involved at every step of the way.

✓ Register early with grants.gov.

✓ Make sure you have the proper software not only on your computer but on the computers of everyone who is involved so they can view the application in process.

✓ Consultants sound expensive; consultants can be worth the money. Carefully vet anyone you consider.

✓ Reporting is a burden but, especially at a small institution, can be worth it.

✓ Make contact with program officers. They may be very helpful, somewhat helpful or absolutely clueless, but you have to find out for yourself. In many agencies, they're assigned by state as well as program (Department of Education).

✓ Make room for all the paperwork. Keep thorough records of all group meetings, says Frazier, noting, "I have kept these when no administrative assistant was available."

Source: Lynne McKenna Frazier, Director of Corporate and Foundation Relations, University of St. Francis, Fort Wayne, IN. Phone (260) 399-7700, ext 6401. E-mail: lfrazier@sf.edu

Gather Boilerplate Materials for Foundation Grant Proposals

Regardless of what your grant proposal is for, you should gather several boilerplate materials that some foundations may ask you to include and keep them in an electronic folder labeled grant boilerplate, says Alice L. Ferris, ACFRE, a partner at GoalBusters Consulting, LLC (Flagstaff, AZ).

These boilerplate materials should include, she says:

• Your mission, vision and values statement if you have one.

• One document that contains a list of all board members' names, addresses and contact information as well as the professional positions of at least the officers.

• A list of principal staff in each project area.

• A signed, electronic copy of your audit. If you are not required to have an audit based on the size of your organization, she says, then have a signed letter stating that on organization letterhead from the board president. "Sometimes a funder will disqualify you if you do not submit an audit," says Ferris. "Rarely, the funder will also want a management letter that

lists recommendations from the auditor and how your management is responding to them."

• Your full Form 990, with all attachments, signed by an officer. "Some funders won't accept it as an official return unless it is signed," she says.

• Your 501(c)(3) (tax exemption) letter.

• A corporate certificate that states you are a corporation in good standing and you are up-to-date on your filings with your state agency. You can get this certificate for a nominal fee. "In some cases the funder will accept a print out of the web page that indicates that you are a corporation in good standing," she says.

• Both your organizational and department budgets. "You want to be able to provide the funder with the budget that is most relevant to the grant request, so when you can and when it is permitted, just submit the department budget and only submit the overall organizational budget depending on the funder's request," she says.

Source: Alice L. Ferris, ACFRE, Partner, GoalBusters Consulting, LLC, Flagstaff, AZ. Phone (888) 883-2690. E-mail: alice.ferris@goalbusters.net

Foundation & Corporate Grants: How to Improve Your Funded Grants Batting Average

DOING YOUR HOMEWORK — RESEARCH

The time you put into early research and planning will not only help you to work more efficiently but will also improve the likelihood of grants success. It pays to become familiar with those foundations/corporations that most closely match your organization's mission and funding priorities. Whether it's studying a foundation's 990-PF or reviewing other charities' donor lists or learning more about individual foundations' and corporations' recent grants, it's critical that you put sufficient time into planning and research before drafting any proposals. The last thing you want to do is chase funds that are incompatible with your organization's strategic direction or to promise something you cannot deliver.

Get to Know Foundation Boards

"It's not what you know, it's who you know."

That maxim is especially true for persons seeking foundation grants, because while simply knowing members of a foundation's board may not lead to a grant, it can greatly improve the odds of securing foundation support.

Once you identify foundations whose giving guidelines you meet, exhaust every opportunity to establish links with any of their board members:

- Review foundation resources that list board of directors' names and other key information (e.g., city of residence, other boards on which they serve, family information, occupation) that may provide clues to help establish a link with your organization.

- Share foundation board members' names with your board and other key friends of your charity to determine if they are acquainted with the contacts or know someone who is.

Although most foundation guidelines advise submitting written requests through the executive director or foundation president, side plays are often made by persons connected to both the charity and someone on the foundation board. While these persons may be told "all requests are handled through our executive director," such contacts will generally accomplish more good than harm if a genuine relationship exists between foundation board members and the persons calling on them on behalf of your cause.

Get to Know Gift Committee Before Making Request

At many businesses, the responsibility for gift decisions goes to a contributions committee made up of representatives from various departments. And often, the method for deciding who gets what is the result of the committee meeting periodically to review gift or grant requests. No one-on-one presentations are permitted.

If this is the case for a corporation you're approaching, take the time to first identify members of gift committees and determine whether any of your contacts (board members, volunteers, etc.) know any of them. Encourage those contacts to do some research on their own and tactfully put in a good word with the committee members they know. What they learn may even impact the type of proposal you submit.

Then, when it comes time to submit your proposal, you will know you have done everything possible to get a favorable response.

How to Get Your Foot In a 'Closed' Foundation's Door

Trying to get your foot in the door at a foundation that says it is closed to anyone but its current list of nonprofits? Try this strategy suggested by Dede Whiteside, a development consultant (San Francisco, CA):

"Find out who the foundation has funded in the past, particularly with multiple gifts, and see if there is anyone in your circle of supporters who knows someone at those organiza-tions who could introduce you to their program officer. If your mission is different than that organization's, it's more likely that they won't see the introduction as competitive, and the foundation's program officer may appreciate the collaborative nature of the approach and at least give you a look."

Source: Dede Whiteside, Development Consultant, Tiberon, CA. Phone (415) 789-0888. E-mail: dedewhiteside@aol.com

Be Privy to a Family Foundation's Extended Family

Many family foundations are closed to unsolicited inquiries. The family chooses which organizations to support based on personal contact or experiences with those organizations. A family member may have a friend who serves on a particular organization's board; read about an interesting organization in the newspaper; or have made personal contributions to a particular organization that he/she would like to support on a larger scale.

So how can an official who feels his/her organization's mission fits with the foundation's core values get a foot in the door? One way is to find a foundation family member who has had a connection to your organization, either as a volunteer, donor or as a friend of a volunteer or donor. The family member will be able to lobby on your organization's behalf when you decide to approach the foundation for a gift.

This approach can be effective even if the family member isn't on the foundation's board. A spokesperson for one private foundation says they sometimes call a family meeting to choose from a group of organizations to support.

Tighten Corporate Profiles

Q. Our corporate profiles are several pages long and we've been asked by our corporate and foundation relations officers to shorten them. Where do we begin? What essential elements do we keep?

"Start by asking your corporate and foundation relations officers what information they find useful. Shorter is better, and most of the focus should be on direct ties to your university or community. As an end-user of such profiles, I want to know:

❑ "What have they previously funded, philanthropic or otherwise?

❑ "Which of our alumni work there, especially in key management or research positions?

❑ "What other points of contact have they had with the university (e.g. advisory boards, committees, development)?

❑ "What types of relationships have they had with the university through non-academic areas?

❑ "If they have a formal giving program (e.g. direct giving, corporate foundation or other), who are the key contacts? What is the application process?

❑ "What and how much do they fund?

❑ "If they haven't funded the university, what other universities have they funded? For what types of projects/programs? Do we have those projects/programs?"

— Kurt R. Moore, Assistant Vice President for Research, Florida Atlantic University (Boca Raton, Fl.)

Measure Likelihood to Give

Prioritizing major gift prospects includes sizing up a foundation's financial capability as well as inclination to give. To help judge a foundation's philanthropic proclivity:

1. **Attempt to learn where the foundation has given in the past (and, if possible, how much).** This will give you a general sense of the foundation's propensity to give. You can assume, for instance, that a foundation that gives generously to 10 organizations will have a higher proclivity to give than a foundation that supports only two organizations.

2. **Measure the degree of connectedness the foundation has to your charity.** Does the foundation have a history of giving to your organization or to similar organizations? Has the foundation benefitted from your organization's services in any way? Does the foundation share the same basic philosophy? To what degree has the foundation been involved with your charity?

What You Can Learn From a Foundation's 990-PF

The IRS requires all private foundations to file tax returns (990-PF forms) on an annual basis, and to make these forms available to the public.

Philanthropic Research, Inc. (PRI) and the Urban Institute's National Center for Charitable Statistics (NCCS) began posting these forms on the Internet (http://www.guidestar.org and http://nccs.urban.org) in March 2000. Keep in mind that the filing period for the forms is such that the most current information you can get is sometimes almost two years old. Each year's form is also just a snapshot of what the foundation has done for that year. Looking at forms over a period of several years, along with the current guidelines and most recent annual report, will give you a better idea of the direction and goals of the foundation.

Although these forms have always been public documents, foundations have been given a mandate to make them available on demand. Posting them on the Internet helps both the foundations and the organizations seeking funds. The forms are still available in print format through the Foundation Center and its cooperating collections, from the IRS, or directly from the foundations, but the ease of access through the Internet makes it even more important for organizations to understand how to interpret these forms. Here are some key things to look for:

- **Contact information** — this gives you the full and proper name of the foundation, along with the mailing address and telephone number. Always check with the foundation to make sure this information has not changed since the form was filed.

- **Fair Market Value of Assets** (*just below the address*) — a good indication of the size of the foundation, which should give you an idea of how much money they give away each year (usually 2-5 percent of assets).

- **Analysis of Changes in Net Assets or Fund Balances** (*Part 3*) — a guide to whether the foundation is growing or declining in assets, and at what rate.

- **Personnel Information** (*Part 8*) — lists directors, trustees, foundation managers, along with the top five highest-paid employees and independent contractors and their compensation. This can be very helpful in determining if you have a connection with any of the key foundation people. It can also help if you are researching the assets and philanthropic interests of the individuals.

- **Supplementary Information** (*Part 15*) — includes contributions by foundation managers, the appropriate contact person for applications, submission formatting and deadlines, and grant restrictions. This information can also be found in most foundation directories and in the guidelines published by the foundation. In addition, this section lists grants and contributions paid during the year and pledges approved for future payment. Use this as an indication of the foundation's priorities and giving ranges. These listings do not always give details of the specific programs that were funded, but the types and locations of recipients can be a guide.

- **Relationships with Noncharitable Tax-Exempt Organizations** (*Part 17*) — lists other organizations with which the foundation has connections. This can lead you to other links and give you more background on the foundation.

All private foundations are required to file tax returns (990-PF forms) on an annual basis, and to make these forms available to the public.

Content not available in this edition

Take Steps to Match Grant Requests With Right Grant Maker

How would staff with a domestic violence shelter in Iowa or a humane society in Alaska or a private school in Texas go about determining which foundations throughout the United States might be interested in making a grant to their organization?

What process or procedure would they follow for sorting out potential grantors?

Deborah S. Koch, director of grants, Springfield Technical Community College (Springfield, MA), says grant makers consistently report the primary reason for grant proposal rejection is that what is being proposed isn't a good match with the funder's stated goals, preferences and limitations.

"You can write the most eloquent proposal about a very well-designed project, but if you send it to the wrong grant maker, you will not get funded," she says.

The initial assessment about a potential grant maker can be made from information posted in a grant-seeking database, says Koch. One database that can be accessed for free is The Foundation Center's Foundation Directory Online.

Log on to http://foundationcenter.org/collections/ to find a cooperating collection in your region.

Koch recommends asking the following questions to determine if the proposed project, the organization and the grant maker are a good match:

- ❑ Is the organization an eligible applicant?
- ❑ Is the organization within the funder's preferred or restricted geographic area?
- ❑ Is the work in alignment with the funder's stated subject matter interests?
- ❑ Is the amount of money requested appropriate for that funder?
- ❑ Does the organization's problem-solving approach and point of view match the funder's?

"Once a potential foundation is identified from a database, review that funder's material directly," she says. "If a foundation does not have a website, call and request the most recent annual report, grant guidelines and list of grants made."

Koch shares this additional advice for choosing potential funders:

- ❑ **Read everything fully.** "The funder is saying who it is; listen carefully because this information can be used to craft the proposal," she says. "Pay attention to the foundation's history, mission statement, vision statements, staff and trustees. Look at the president's and executive director's annual report letters for any indicator of the direction that they intend their foundation to go; sometimes you can learn things this way that you might not otherwise know. Inspect the foundation's tax return (called a 990-PF) to see a list of grants made and list of the board of directors. Gather information about the foundation from general news articles, philanthropic media and listservs where your peers may post findings."

- ❑ **Look at what a grant maker says, but also look at what it does.** "Grants made are a good indicator of what the funder values," Koch says. When examining the list of grants awarded, ask these questions:

  - ✓ Does the grant maker demonstrate that it funds what it says it does?
  - ✓ Does it correspond in method to our project or organization's approach?
  - ✓ Does the grant maker fund organizations like ours?
  - ✓ Does it fund a lot of activities like those in our project?

Finally, Koch says, investigate from where organizations such as yours are getting their funding.

"Plug the name of your organizational associates into a grants database to see what funder names come up," she says. "This is a very quick way to determine grant maker preferences and to assure yourself that your activities would be appealing to them."

Sources: Deborah S. Koch, Director of Grants, Springfield Technical Community College; Grant Consultant, Kochworks, Easthampton, MA. Phone (413) 586-2092. E-mail: kochworks@yahoo.com

Foundation Scouting Tips

- ■ When you come across biographies of other foundations' members, pay attention. See if any information about them matches your funding projects in specific or mission in general. Then look for ways to connect the person and your cause.

Make Time to Review Other Charities' Donor Lists

The world of competitive intelligence is not limited to corporations and countries. Nonprofits can benefit from a little research into what their competition is up to, especially regarding their donors. And it's all legal, ethical, and above board. Whether your organization is a large university or a small social service agency, here are some things to keep in mind when you're checking out other charities:

Collecting the Lists
Gather event programs and invitations. These generally include lists of underwriters, supporters and committees, and you can collect them directly from the charities by asking for copies. Your own staff, board and volunteers may also receive copies by attending events or by being invited to support other organizations. Make it known to them that you are collecting these items.

Newspaper, radio, and television advertising can be another useful source of information. Many organizations officially thank their supporters before, during, or after events, or as part of campaign marketing. The lists may just have major supporters or may name everyone down to the donors of gift certificates to their auctions. This information may even be available on their websites.

Get on the mailing lists of other charities so you can receive their newsletters and magazines. A number of non-profits publish honor rolls of their donors in these vehicles on a regular basis.

Collect annual reports from other organizations. Along with the financial information, these generally include major supporters, committee members and board listings.

Analyzing the Lists
A useful piece of information is the type of event being put on by the charities. Donors to golf tournaments may be quite different from those who would support a season at the symphony.

Categorize your list collection. Break it down into whatever categories work for you, looking for those charities similar to your own as well as those with different constituencies. You can sort them by location, type (education, social-service, arts, etc.) or even competitors vs. noncompetitors.

Take a look at the types of donors listed. Does the charity list mostly corporate or foundation support, or are individuals included?

Investigate the donor levels. They may be categorized just

by group names such as patron or they may actually list dollar amounts for the various levels. Invitations will usually include amounts whereas programs and listings after the events may not. Obviously, knowing the actual amount the donors gave will be better, but generic rankings can also be helpful.

Try to identify the type of support given by the donors. This would include underwriting (generally cash), in-kind (such as printing, food, entertainment) and auction items. Some donors may participate in several categories.

Board and committee lists are useful, too. Check to see if the individuals on these lists are also donors or just providing volunteer time and expertise.

Using the Lists
If at all possible, set up a database to track the information you find in the lists you collect. It may just be a set of fields or a screen in your regular donor database, or it may be a separate system. Track the type of organization, amount, and date of the donations. If you know the type of donation (underwriting, in-kind, or auction), include that, too. This information can help you compile new lists when you are looking for specific types and groups of donors for your own events and campaigns. It also provides a more manageable way to access the data than sorting through stacks of programs, reports and honor rolls.

Compare your organization to similar charities, events and donor categories as a way of seeing how you rank in the marketplace.

When you are trying to find donors for corporate event underwriters, foundation support, auction items, etc., use the lists to help you target new prospects.

Knowing that your current donors give to other organizations, and at what level they give, can also be helpful when you are determining your strategy to solicit them again.

Tracking the frequency of donations made by your prospects and current donors to other organizations can also aid you in timing your solicitations.

When searching for individuals to serve on your boards and committees, look at those who are serving other organizations. This is a two-sided issue. You don't want to always tap into the same group as other charities, but knowing that someone is committed to philanthropy and volunteerism for another cause is a good indication he or she might be a possibility for your non-profit.

Look at Giving History When Researching Foundations

When researching foundations, it's important to look beyond their stated interests and restrictions to take a close look at giving history, which may reveal broader priorities, says Christina Pulawski, an independent consultant with Christina Pulawski Consulting (Chicago, IL).

Pulawski says that often, an organization's giving history is based on the interests of its board members or other leaders.

"As tacky as it sounds, I used to keep a liar's list of foundations that would fund outside of their stated interests, usually due to the interest of a board member," the independent consultant says.

This practice might indicate the presence of a discretionary fund for grants that can be used to fund a favorite organization or to allow a particular board member or family member to direct the funds, she says. Sometimes, she notes, foundations will provide funding to a location outside their designated geographic area because a board member happens to live at the location or for another such reason.

Once she identified a foundation that funded outside of its stated interests and restrictions, she says, "I would then focus on finding a way for our organization to connect with that foundation's leadership."

Source: Christina Pulawski, Principal, Christina Pulawski Consulting, Chicago, IL. Phone (773) 255-3873. E-mail: c-pulawski@comcast.net

Don't Be Shy About Making a Phone Call

You've discovered a foundation that might make a good match with your nonprofit. You have visited with other grant recipients and read everything available about the foundation's funding guidelines, annual report and more.

Now what? Simply write and submit a proposal? Wrong. Unless the guidelines say no phone calls, pick up the phone and make an introductory call.

The personal touch can actually help to begin a relationship-building process. Equally important, an initial phone call can give you insight into next steps: submitting a letter, scheduling a meeting with a foundation officer or simply moving ahead with your proposal.

Don't be a victim of phone phobia. Make that call to pave the way for a successful grant.

How to Approach Foundations for Significant Gifts

Although the process of cultivating a relationship with a foundation is much like nurturing a relationship with an individual, there are some key differences in the steps you might take:

1. **Identify the key decision makers.** Unlike an individual, foundations sometimes have a gift committee or a particular position that is key in the decision-making process. The company may or may not have written funding guidelines you should follow.

2. **Determine the company's funding interests.** Find out about past gifts the company has made to other charitable causes. Company officials may share this information if asked, or you may need to do some research by reviewing annual reports or examining lists of contributors to various nonprofit organizations. What projects were funded? What benefits, such as recognition, did the company receive as a result of the gift or grant? Differentiate past outright gifts as opposed to sponsorships.

3. **Determine timing decisions.** Are gift decisions made on a yearly, quarterly or random basis? Are those timing decisions tied to company budgeting decisions?

4. **Turn to your board or current donors for help.** Who among your organization's constituents might be close to any of the company's key decision makers? Ask for their help in determining the best approach to take.

5. **Offer benefits that appeal to foundations.** Companies often make funding decisions that will further their corporate image. Be mindful of recognition that might appeal to a foundation rather than an individual.

How to Find the Best Corporate, Foundation Prospects

The best way to gauge the interest level of a foundation or corporation, determine its capacity to give a major gift, affinity to your organization and interest in your programs, says Christina Pulawski, an independent consultant with Christina Pulawski Consulting (Chicago, IL).

"Does that corporation or foundation give its funds in the type of chunks that you need?" she says. "For example, if you need $100,000, and the foundation gives a maximum of $100,000, but in smaller amounts of $20,000, that foundation does not have the capacity to fund your project, or you will need to adjust your approach."

You can determine the prospect's affinity to your organization by looking at what ties the corporation or foundation has with your program. Do you have board members in common? Someone who can make an introduction? Are there other natural partners?

"The best organizational prospects are those with natural ties to your mission or goals, and that basically want the same outcomes your organization is trying to accomplish," she says. "They should also have an interest in your specific programs, and have strong ties to your community and constituency."

The goal of your initial research should be to come up with a short list of prospects, says Pulawski. "At this stage, a print-out of what your organization does with a justification of why the funder is a good match should be enough to help decide whether to move forward or invest more time in building a relationship," she says. "You will also want to involve your organization's staff to find out who among them has ties to the corporate or foundation prospects on your list.

"Remember, building strong and long-term relationships with organizational funders is just as important as building donor relationships in individual fundraising — and should be planned accordingly," she says. "Sometimes the only difference is giving motivation or the approach method."

Your in-depth research will take place when you are actually preparing the proposal, she says: "That's when you make the most of your database, evaluate your connections to determine the best initial approach, look at your giving history, and research your off-the-shelf material (such as foundation directories), as well as conduct a thorough analysis of the foundation or corporation's prior relationship and giving history to see how it matches up with what your funding and timing needs are."

Source: Christina Pulawski, Principal, Christina Pulawski Consulting, Chicago, IL. Phone (773) 255-3873. E-mail: c-pulawski@comcast.net

---

Be Proactive About Prospect Research

General prospect research should be an ongoing, proactive activity, says Christina Pulawski, an independent consultant with Christina Pulawski Consulting (Chicago, IL).

"The ability to be proactive comes from knowing your organization — its program and needs — and who your leadership connections are, and constantly mining them for whom they might know that might have a tie to a grant-making organization," she says.

Keep an eye on organizations similar to yours and who is funding them so that you can make sure they are in the queue for an approach from you, says Pulawski.

She shares other ways you can be proactive when conducting general prospect research:

- **Build on a known relationship.** You might have a lot of grant makers who haven't funded you to the extent of their abilities. Take a close look at who is funding your organization and where you are on their hierarchy of giving. Are you at the top or the bottom? If you are at the bottom, why are you? Is it because you have not cultivated those interests as much? You want to make sure your funders are funding you at their capacity to give to you.

- **Focus your efforts.** If you know a project needs funding — or if you anticipate general funding needs in a particular area — identify a short list of funders whose interest and capacity might lead them to consider giving you a grant or initiating a cooperative relationship.

- **Prepare and present a proposal.** Once you have a known funder and project, make sure the proposal carefully follows specific guidelines and has the subtleties that will click all the triggers to be a success.

Make Your Project Attractive to Funders

When you are trying to convince a foundation to invest in your organization, you will need to tell them why the funding project is important to your community, how it will contribute to your mission, and how people's lives will be affected as a result of the new program, says Alice L. Ferris, ACFRE, a partner at GoalBusters Consulting, LLC (Flagstaff, AZ).

"The whys are important because you don't necessarily want to seek grants for a project that is peripheral to your organization," she says.

Ferris shares the four main things a grant funder will look for in your grant proposal:

1. **A request for restricted funds.** "The majority of funders are going to be looking for restricted projects," she says. "A couple of U.S. foundations have recently revised their grant proposal guidelines to include general operating funds because of today's economy, but generally those foundations are limiting those gifts to organizations they have funded before."

2. **Start-up or early stage projects.** "Typically foundations don't want to come into a project that is well-established or that seems to be doing fine," she says. "That's more like general operating to them. The caveat to that is if you have a project that has been well established but you are going through a modification or expansion to it. Otherwise, generally funders are most attracted to the stage when you're on the cusp of really taking off."

3. **A request for funding that doesn't exceed three years.** "Funders don't want to give you a grant beyond three years, and most don't want to fund beyond one to two years," she says. "Funders want to know how you are going to sustain this program financially beyond their granting period, showing the new income streams that will be coming in after their grant ends. They tend to get nervous when your funding will depend on their grant for an extended period."

4. **A clear and measurable impact.** "As much as you can find things that you can measure, and find things that are quantifiable, do so, but don't make busy work for yourself," she says. "If it's not something you're going to measure, or be useful to measure internally, don't do it just because you think you can turn it into a proposal."

Source: Alice L. Ferris, ACFRE, Partner, GoalBusters Consulting, LLC, Flagstaff, AZ. Phone (888) 883-2690. E-mail: alice.ferris@goalbusters.net

Define Projects Before Drafting Grant Proposals

Although planning grant requests may take more time than actually writing the proposal, it's the most important part of the grant-writing process.

First, define what you want the funded project to accomplish (your project goals).

Next, come up with key objectives required to achieve that goal (or multiple goals). List who will benefit from the realization of this funding project and in what ways (project outcomes).

Finally, produce a timetable that outlines the planning period, the time required to identify likely grant sources, proposal production deadlines and the intended project start date.

This planning period will legitimize the steps that follow.

Use the table at right to help formulate your own grant request plan.

Content not available in this edition

Foundation & Corporate Grants: How to Improve Your Funded Grants Batting Average

CREATE SYSTEMS TO PRIORITIZE, MANAGE AND TRACK PROSPECTS

How do you decide which foundations are worth pursuing for a grant? How do you go about identifying and prioritizing your organization's funding opportunities? This chapter will give you insight into how to establish systems and procedures to help manage and track your foundation/corporate grants efforts. You can develop an organized system based on: funders, pending proposals, in-progress proposals, prospects, past funders and rejected proposals.

Develop a Priority System for Foundation Proposals

How do you go about determining which foundation proposals get written and submitted first?

Here are three criteria that make sense for prioritizing proposal order:

1. **Program justification.** How important is the realization of the project in light of your mission and existing programs?

2. **Budgetary impact.** Will the realization of the grant provide budget relief. Or will it place greater obligations on the budget?

3. **Fundraising potential.** How compelling would a foundation find the project to be? Would it compete with other fundraising endeavors?

This three-pronged approach to proposal production will help to focus attention on top funding opportunities.

Create a System for Grant-writing Requests

Odds of receiving corporate and foundation grants increase proportionately based on the number of written requests you have pending. To develop several requests, establish a timetable such as this that coincides deadlines of foundations you wish to approach:

Plus-12 Weeks in Advance:	Conduct basic research on the foundation.
10 to 12 Weeks in Advance:	Send a letter of inquiry to the foundation.
Six to Eight Weeks in Advance:	Call for an initial interview with the aim of receiving an annual report, giving guidelines and an expression of interest in your project.
Four to Six Weeks in Advance:	Conduct a preliminary interview with the funding source to review potential funding opportunities including the project, program, staffing and/or equipment you will propose.
Two to Three Weeks in Advance:	Draft the proposal.
NOW:	Funding source's deadline for receiving proposals.
One Week After:	Conduct a follow-up call to make sure all necessary information was received.
Two Weeks Later:	Follow-up visit (if possible).
Two Weeks to Nine Months Later:	Receipt of the funding source's decision.

Have a System for Tracking Foundation Proposals

Establishing a simple but effective system to track important tasks can help improve your ability to accomplish goals and free up time for more important duties.

Hester Bury, grants manager, Northern Illinois Food Bank (St. Charles, IL), uses a simple Microsoft Excel document called a Grant Calendar to track the status of her foundation gift proposals.

"I look at the grant calendar every day to make sure I know how to prioritize projects," says Bury. "It helps me to track whom we have heard from and whom we haven't so that I can follow up."

The calendar tracks proposals by due date or deadline. Since many foundation grant deadlines are on the first of the month, Bury puts those on her calendar at the end of the current month to give her a two- or three-week heads-up.

In addition, the calendar tracks the following information on each proposal:

- Type of grant or LOI (letter of interest).
- How they learned of the grant.
- Foundation to which grant was submitted.
- What type of grant the proposal is for (e.g., general operating, youth program, senior program).
- What type of past support the foundation has given.
- How much the proposal asks for this time.

- The date the proposal was submitted.
- The date the food bank was notified of the decision.
- The amount received or denied.
- Any site visits or face-to-face visits with foundation representatives.

Outstanding grant applications are listed in bold type, and switched to normal type as soon as they are submitted. Accepted proposals are highlighted in a different color than denied ones. Once a decision is received, Bury puts the grant on the calendar for the next date that the foundation is accepting proposals (usually the same time each year).

Source: Hester Bury, Grants Manager, Northern Illinois Food Bank, St. Charles, IL. Phone (630) 443-6910, ext. 24. E-mail: Hbury@northernilfoodbank.org

---

Online Links to Grants

Online resources can be invaluable in identifying funding opportunities. Here are four websites that help guide you to your next grant:

- Fundsnet Services Online: www.fundsnetservices.com
- The Grantsmanship Center: www.tgci.com
- GrantStation: www.grantstation.com
- Resource Associates: The Grant Experts: www.grantwriters.net

---

Organize Grant Proposals

The key to juggling several grant proposals is staying organized.

"There is so much competition for grants these days," says Wendy Smith, independent development consultant (Highland Park, IL). "If you make one error, it could exclude you from receiving funding that year. It's absolutely critical to stay on top of everything that needs to be done."

She suggests the following tips:

- **Utilize spreadsheets.** "There are two critical pieces that can help keep you organized," says Smith. "One is a general spreadsheet and the other is a separate spreadsheet for each program/project you're trying to fund." The general spreadsheet details each proposal submitted, including: foundation name; submission date; the expected response; what the proposal requested; the response; the effective funding date, if received; due dates for required reports; date the next proposal can be submitted; and contact persons. The other ia a spreadsheet for each program/project you are trying to fund. Include possible funding sources and their beginning/end dates, so you can track when fund

sources are diminishing and how much needs to be raised.

- **Manage a separate calendar.** "Have a separate calendar for report due dates," says Smith. "Two weeks before a due date, mark on your calendar that it needs to be completed." Smith also emphasizes it's important to check the calendar and database constantly.

- **Back up information and databases.** "Consider using an online database, such as eTapestry (www.eTapestry.com), so there is no risk of losing your information," says Smith. In addition to securing your information, online databases allow anyone from your organization to access the database from any location.

Smith suggests keeping files with all records, source information and personal notes from conversations. She also suggests following up with any declination and taking notes.

Source: Wendy S. Smith, CFRE, Independent Development Consultant, Highland Park, IL. Phone (847) 831-2309. E-mail: wendySsmith@comcast.net

Grid System Prioritizes Funding Sources

The process of narrowing down and prioritizing funding sources provides much greater focus in identifying and pursuing foundation and corporation grants. This prospect prioritization grid can be a useful tool to help you in this important process.

✓ To begin, it's important to know your organization's needs and develop a sense of funding priorities. For instance, is library renovation more important than new science labs? The ability to categorize needs will help to know which projects to pursue most rigorously. You may want to form a grants committee to collectively prioritize funding needs. Those projects receiving "A" ratings, for instance, are of highest priority, while those with "C" ratings are desirable, but least important.

✓ Once you identify your funding needs, initiate an ongoing commitment to review publications and periodicals publicizing foundation and corporate grants.

✓ After reviewing publications best addressing your interests, list the foundations/corporations whose grants are in line with the funding projects you wish to pursue.

✓ If available, include the names of one or two organizations that received funding in case you choose to contact them for further information.

✓ Finally, check those categories matching the foundation or corporate grant with the appropriate organizational needs.

This grid helps focus funding efforts on foundations and corporations most closely related to your organization's specific needs and programs.

Content not available in this edition

Track Your Top 50 Corporate Prospects

As important as it is to track cultivation/solicitation activity of individual prospects, it's equally important to track top corporate prospects. And because key activities surrounding corporate prospects can differ from those for individuals, using software or a form such as the example shown here is a useful tool for corporate gifts managers.

First, identify and prioritize your top 50 corporate prospects by reviewing past donor files, conducting rating and screening sessions among staff, board members and other volunteers and by other means.

Once you identify your top 50 corporate prospects based on capability and inclination to give, plan and monitor all cultivation and solicitation moves monthly. This collective view of activities surrounding your top 50 will help in the overall solicitation of these key prospects.

Create and utilize a form such as this to track top corporate prospects.

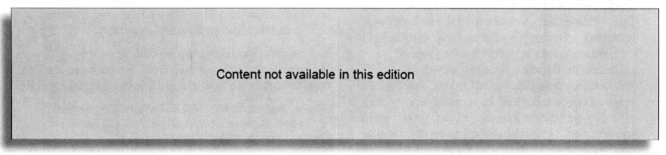

Content not available in this edition

Report System Helps Monitor Status of Proposals and Grants

To expand your pool of potential grant funders — and stay on top of existing grants' statuses — a monthly grant report helps track both prospects and grantors.

A monthly grant report system shouldn't require much explanation, it is most practical for each organization to develop their own use for it. The basis of this form, however, includes a system for dividing funders among categories — current funders with contracts, pending proposals, in-progress, prospects, past funders, and rejected proposals.

The form should be completed monthly. Implementing the system will take the most work with monthly revisions. The system also allows the organization to evaluate and measure funders and potential funders and helps generate action steps to be assigned.

Goals for implementing a grant report system include improving prospects and relationships with each individual funder and potential funder, and increasing the number of continuing funders.

Grant Monitoring Report Information

Funder — name, address, phone, key contact(s)

Field — state government, nonprofit, children's welfare, consortium, etc.

Source — how did we first learn of this organization and make first contact?

PS — prospects for contract in the short-term — next 3 to 12 months — rate on a scale of 1 to 4: 1=poor, 2=fair, 3=good, 4=excellent

PL — prospects for the long-term — next 12 months — rate on a scale of 1 to 4: 1=poor, 2=fair, 3=good, 4=excellent

QOR — quality of relationship with key contact and organization — rate on a scale of 1 to 4: 1=poor, 2=fair, 3=good, 4=excellent

Past contracts — dollar amount

Current contracts — dollar amount

Future financial support — anticipated

Remarks — action items to improve scores on measurable items and move funder up the ladder to a current funder

Funder Categories

A. **Funders** — current funders with contracts, best source of future business either as continued funder for existing projects or new projects, or can help with referrals and positive goodwill through word of mouth. Highest priority is to do an outstanding job with strong customer relations.

B. **Pending Proposals** — proposals submitted or in negotiation process. Must be able to respond with answer to every question, do everything possible to expedite process, be available to answer questions. Either will become an existing funder or a rejected proposal. Goal will be to increase success rate by submitting quality competitive proposals based on cost and content. Need to increase success rate, chance of successful proposal.

C. **In-Progress** — made the decision to submit a proposal. Using timeline for deadlines and assignments.

D. **Prospects** — possible new funders, information gathering. Identify key contact, understand competition, formal RFP, certification as contractor.

E. **Past Funders** — possible source of new business, referral and reference. Need to maintain regular contact, follow-up mailing. These funders might be getting requests for information about your project or similar projects. Encourage wide distribution of reports from past work.

F. **Rejected Proposals** — follow up to see why they failed, use information for next similar proposal, stay in touch on at least an annual basis with call or note. Understand and analyze the competition: Successful competitor might fail, new bid process be in a better position, have already done some of the work preparing proposal, project might be broken up from non-conformance by current contractor, might have other related work. Might want to contact successful bidder for possible sub-contract.

Content not available in this edition

Corporate Sponsorship Commitment Form Helps Track Sponsorships

Special Events and Corporate Sponsorship Manager Beth Hrubesky uses this corporate sponsorship commitment form to help her keep track of several special events held both locally and regionally in support of the Girls Scouts of the Northwestern Great Lakes, Inc. (Green Bay, WI).

"It's best to take the form in and talk to sponsors in person," Hrubesky says. "If that is not possible, we mail the form with a letter that makes reference to a mutual friend. Each prospective sponsor receives a follow-up phone call by someone who believes in our mission."

The first page of the four-page form includes information about the event. For example, the "Women of Courage, Confidence and Character" sponsorship commitment form describes the event and includes photos of the girls the event supports. The second and third pages outline the benefits the sponsor will receive.

The fourth page of the form collects sponsors' contact information and the level of sponsorship they are choosing. It also includes an area for them to indicate whether they have enclosed a check; will be mailing it, and by what date; or want to be billed.

"When a sponsor pays depends on the time of year and their budget," says Hrubesky. "We let them choose when to write out the check. I have never had a sponsor confirm their sponsorship and not pay."

The forms allow Hrubesky to track the number of sponsors for each event, and where they are in the process. Once a signed form is received, for example, a sponsor is moved from the verbal commitment category to confirmed (if accompanied by a check) and pending if not. All sponsors must have a completed and signed form on file, she says.

A thank-you letter is sent to sponsors upon receipt of each signed form.

"If they checked the box on the form that says they will pay by X date, and they have not, I may send another thank-you letter as a way to prompt them to make payment," says Hrubesky. "I never come out and ask directly for payment. I prefer to take the softer approach."

After each event, Hrubesky follows up with a handwritten note to each sponsor.

Source: Beth Hrubesky, Special Events and Corporate Sponsorship Manager, Girl Scouts of the Northwestern Great Lakes, Inc., Green Bay Service Center, Green Bay, WI.
Phone (920) 469-4860, ext. 4013.
E-mail: BHrubesky@gsnwgl.org

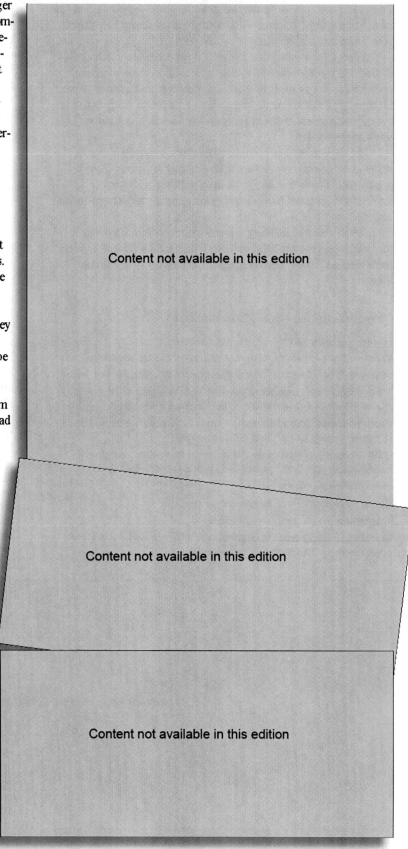

Content not available in this edition

Foundation & Corporate Grants: How to Improve Your Funded Grants Batting Average

FOLLOW GUIDELINES AND APPLICATION PROCEDURES

To receive the highest level of consideration from foundations and corporations, it's imperative that you adhere to their submission guidelines. Those guidelines will address procedures such as: submission deadlines, eligibility, proposal format, review procedures and funding timetable, required budget information, goals and priorities and awards levels.

Clarify Foundation Guidelines

Most foundations will publish guidelines to help you decide if it's worth the time and effort to submit a grant proposal. Some guidelines are found on the foundation's website; others can be requested and received by mail.

Once secured, a foundation's guidelines should address these topics:

1. Submission deadlines
2. Eligibility
3. Proposal format (e.g., contents, pages, additional materials required, etc.)
4. Review and funding timetable
5. Needed budget information
5. Funding goals and priorities
6. Award levels
7. Evaluation process and criteria
8. Who to contact

> **Online Guideline Examples**
>
> Below are examples of foundations that offer online guidelines:
>
> **Ben & Jerry's Foundation**
> www.benandjerrysfoundation.org
>
> **The Coca-Cola Foundation**
> www.thecoca-colacompany.com/
> citizenship/application_guidelines.html
>
> **Glazer Family Foundation**
> www.glazerfamilyfoundation.com/
> GuidelinesforGrants.aspx

Grant Proposal Guidelines

Although proposals vary by project and foundation, these 11 basic grant proposal guidelines will boost your odds of success:

1. **Follow funders' directions.** Note deadlines, formats, contacts and program limitations.

2. **Include a concise cover letter** printed on your nonprofit's letterhead.

3. **Provide an executive summary** — a one-page summary of amount requested, grant's purpose, total budget for the project and anticipated outcome of the funded project.

4. **List a table of contents.** Include major sections and appendices.

5. **Use headings and subheadings.** Break the document into smaller sections which are logically arranged.

6. **State project goals.** Be specific and detailed in proposal body. Indicate methods you will use to reach goals.

7. **Include measurable goals.** Know in advance how you will evaluate the effectiveness of the funded project.

8. **Set up a realistic budget.** Include only those items necessary to the immediate project. Be able to justify expenses.

9. **Reveal any additional sources of funds for project use.** State those sources of which you are certain, and indicate if other funders are being approached for the project.

10. **Attach appendices.** Include tax-exempt documents, board listing, project personnel biographies, endorsement letters and any other supporting documents.

11. **Share the proposal before it is submitted.** Edit and proofread the document several times, and get the opinions of colleagues who are not directly involved in the project.

Grant-seeking Advice

Don't be discouraged by foundation search listings that state: "No unsolicited proposals accepted." Many foundations list themselves as such to limit the number of proposals they receive or discourage frivolous, mass-mailed grant requests.

When encountering such statements, your best operating procedure is generally to contact those foundations before attempting to cultivate them. Write a letter or call them on the phone to determine their preferred method of initial contact. Or, if you have a volunteer or board member who is affiliated with a particular foundation, ask that person for help getting your foot in the door.

Land That Foundation Grant

Doing your homework and following instructions remain as important today as when you were in school.

About a quarter of foundation grant proposals are rejected because the grant writers haven't done their homework to make sure their request meets the foundation's funding interests, says Kurt Moore, director of corporate and foundation relations, Florida Atlantic University (Boca Raton, FL). Moore bases that on conversations he has had with foundation program officers over the years.

He says another quarter of requests are rejected because the applicants don't follow the directions completely.

Moore shares six tips for landing your next foundation grant:

1. Make sure your request matches the foundation's funding interests.

2. Follow the proposal directions.

3. Don't be afraid to ask the program officer for clarifications. If you're uncertain about something, don't make assumptions.

4. When writing the proposal, make sure you are communicating effectively. Use clear, concise writing and avoid jargon.

5. When you get to the budget portion of the proposal, make sure your ask is within the foundation's range (toward the middle if this is your first request to this foundation).

6. If it's a longer proposal, include a one-page executive summary that outlines your ask amount, main points and contact information.

Source: Kurt R. Moore, CFRE, Interim Associate Vice President for Advancement, Director of Corporate & Foundation Relations, Florida Atlantic University, Division of University Advancement, Boca Raton, FL. Phone (561) 297-4064. E-mail: kmoore34@fau.edu

Identify Yourself Properly in Grant Applications

Q. "When presenting information about the organization in grant requests, are there any circumstances in which you would include divisional (e.g., College of Education) rather than organization-wide information when filling out that portion of a grant request?"

"The funder is seeking information related to the legal entity that will accept the grant, should one be awarded. In the case of colleges and universities, for example, the only legal entity that may accept the award is the college or university that legally exists. Departments and divisions (or colleges within a university) have no separate, legal standing on their own. Their existence, if you will, derives from their association with the legal entity — the college or university.

"The funder wants the legal entity's articles of incorporation, a list of its board of trustees/overseers, the name of its president/CEO, and the accompanying contact information, as that is the entity that may enter into the legal contract (the grant). This information also demonstrates to the funder that the college or university is aware that a grant proposal has been submitted and reviewed, and that a decision has been made.

"If the grant opportunity is directed toward a specific department, division, college or school within a larger institution, then it is appropriate to also provide the mission/purpose of that school and information about those persons in the school who will deliver the programs/services described in the proposal."

— Susan D. Smith, Consultant, Susan D. Smith Consultant in Philanthropy (Barneveld, NY)

Tips for Dealing With Family Foundations

Q. *"When initially approaching small family foundations, should you put the ask amount in the letter? Also, who should sign the letter?"*

"If you know the foundation's range of giving and giving interests, include the request in the letter. In the case of first-time requests, we often include three or four options we think they may be interested in. We use the president's signature for all foundation asks."

— Marcie McCleary, Director, Foundation Relations, Westminster College, (Salt Lake City, UT)

"We do put the ask in the letter. I think that being up front about what we are hoping to have funded increases the possibility of getting that funding if a full proposal is invited. At least the expectation is out on the table and can be a point of conversation early in the process rather than come as a surprise later. Who signs the letter depends on who (if anyone) has a relationship with the foundation. As a general rule, our vice president of development signs the letter, but it can also be me, our president, or even a dean if there is an existing relationship."

— Cindy E. Hales, Director of Corporate and Foundation Relations, Central Michigan University, (Mount Pleasant, MI)

"I deal exclusively with small family and corporate foundations. Include the amount you are requesting. Foundations want to know right up front, who is asking, how much you want and what you want it for in the first paragraph. The letter should be signed by the organization's president or CEO. The most successful proposals are those that come from the president and CEO. A foundation wants to know the administration is aware of the grant-seeking activities of the organization and in some instances, that the board is involved. Lately I have had requests for the board chair to also sign the letter of intent or the request for funding. It's important to show that the project has the support of the administration at the highest levels."

Mary Egan, Grant Writer/Administrator, Claxton-Hepburn Medical Center, (Ogdensburg, NY)

Grant Applications May Raise Issues of Confidentiality

Q. *"Many grant applications ask for an organization's 10 biggest gifts or all gifts over a certain amount, including names of donors and amount of each gift. Is it a breach of confidentiality to disclose donor names and gift amounts to foundations? What if the donor asked to remain anonymous?"*

"Confidentiality applies only to individual donors and corporate giving programs. However, most companies don't object to anyone publicizing their charitable gifts, since it's good PR for them. Gifts from private and corporate foundations are public record. As nonprofits, they have to report these on their IRS Form 990, which is a public document.

"When a prospective donor asks me for a list of previous gifts, I break out corporate and foundation gifts, but list an aggregate total for individual donors. I explain that individual donors are not listed to protect their privacy or to honor confidentiality requests."

— Dennis Alexander, Director of Foundation Relations, Texas Christian University (Fort Worth, TX)

"There is a confidentiality issue when providing donor names and amounts, but there is also a workable compromise. Many grant applications that request such information usually have smaller nonprofits in mind and want to see that they have support and fiscal stability. A Top 10 list can be crafted easily without betraying confidences. Start with the anonymous gifts and list the amount and date and label these gifts Anonymous. For foundations or other grantors where the information is public record (published if a governmental agency or in the 990s of a foundation) list the amount and date of the gift and the name of the funder.

"For individuals, corporations and other donors, if you have published a report or honor roll, then list gift range (unless you have permission to list exact amount or have announced an exact amount in a press release), date of the gift and donor name. I've never had any problem with a potential funder when listing donors and their gifts in this way."

— Kurt R. Moore, Assistant Vice President for Research, Florida Atlantic University (Boca Raton, FL)

Work Within Parameters When Applying for Federal Grants

Federal grant competitions are extremely competitive, so it's important that grant writers follow all the rules exactly, says Cheryl L. Kester, partner, Thomas-Forbes & Kester Grant Consultants (Fayetteville, AR).

"I know of grant competitions in which the cut-off score for fundable applications was 98.6 out of 100," the grants expert says. "When you are preparing a federal grant application, your every paper has to be an A paper, an extraordinary paper."

Competing for a federal grant, says Kester, is less about where you put each comma and more about religiously answering each and every one of the prompts clearly and thoroughly: "Make sure you follow all the other arcane rules as well, e.g., the CV can only be two pages; charts have to be in 12-point font; you must have a letter from your state office of Rural Health; etc. If you don't know what a logic model is, you can't just leave it out and hope the reviewers don't notice."

Kester says that there is no single silver bullet to winning a federal grant competition since every federal agency is different. "They may offer technical assistance workshops or conference calls, or they may not," she says. "They may have competent staff willing to help you before you submit your proposal, or they may not. They may allow you to single-space inside charts and tables, or they may not, or they may give you conflicting information about whether this is acceptable."

While such variances may be frustrating, she says, it's better to learn to work within the parameters than to expend time and energy fighting them.

Source: Cheryl L. Kester, Partner, Thomas-Forbes & Kester Grants Consultants, Fayetteville, AR. Phone (479) 582-1053. E-mail: ckester@cox.net

Six Steps to Winning Grant Applications

Crafting a winning grant application goes beyond dotting all your I's and crossing all your T's.

Kathy Bangasser, grants officer, Lutheran Social Services of South Dakota (Sioux Falls, SD), recommends grant writers carefully read the request for proposal (RFP) at least twice before doing anything else.

"The first time, highlight the priorities and required activities," says Bangasser. "The second time, in a different color, highlight the technical requirements such as margins, deadlines, etc."

The grants officer shares six additional steps to help increase the odds of grant application success:

1. Follow all the directions to the letter.

2. The RFP will be very specific about the kind of services the organization will fund. Don't try to shoehorn in something else that isn't a good fit.

3. Get registered on the Central Contractor Registry and with grants.gov. This can take from several days to several weeks. An increasing number of RFPs require that proposals be submitted online through grants.gov.

4. Pay careful attention to the evaluation criteria listed in the RFP. Your proposal should clearly address each of the criteria.

5. Early in the planning process, gather matching resources, partners and letters of agreement or memoranda of understanding. These elements will take the most time to gather.

6. Look ahead. Lately, some federal RFPs have come out only a few weeks before the deadline. If you know that an RFP will come out sometime, get your planning started ahead of time rather than waiting for the RFP.

Kathy Bangasser, Grants Officer, Lutheran Social Services of South Dakota, Sioux Falls, SD. Phone (800) 568-2401.

Foundation & Corporate Grants: How to Improve Your Funded Grants Batting Average

INTRODUCING YOURSELF TO FOUNDATIONS, CORPORATIONS

How do you go about making that initial contact with a foundation or corporation? What can you do to capture their attention without being excluded from grant consideration? It's one thing to get your foot in the door; it's another to compete with other worthy causes vying for the same grant dollars.

Know Who and Why When Making Foundation Inroads

While there is no cookie-cutter approach to making introductions to foundations, the No. 1 rule is to know whom you are trying to reach out to and how they like to operate, says Mary Hanifin, executive director of corporate and foundation relations, Brown University (Providence, RI).

"You don't want to alienate someone before you have even had a chance to communicate directly with him or her," Hanifin says. "For example, if a foundation says that the first introduction should come in written form, then that's what you should do."

Once you develop a relationship with certain foundation gift officers, you may have more flexibility in how you approach them a second or third time, she says: "You may be able to pick up the phone and say, 'Remember that program you funded last year? We have another one we think you might be interested in.'"

Don't be afraid to develop relationships with foundation program officers, the fundraising expert adds. After all, you both have assets to bring to the table.

"We empower our staff to think of their work as being the other half of what foundation officers do," says Hanifin. "We are offering a foundation something that they need. We are a resource for them — someone who comes to them with a solution to the problems they have identified. Empowering our staff to think about their work in that way makes them better at their work."

Source: Mary Hanifin, Executive Director of Corporate & Foundation Relations, Brown University, Providence, RI.
Phone (401) 863-3904. E-mail: Mary_Hanifin@brown.edu

Set the Stage for Cold Calls With an Introductory Letter

Veteran development professionals will tell you that the best method for making contact with new prospects is through a mutual introduction by someone close to both the prospect and your organization. As helpful as that method can be, there are obviously times when that cannot occur. In those instances, it's better to attempt a cold call than to make no contact at all.

When it's necessary to make a cold call on a prospect, is it best to show up unannounced, hoping to gain an audience? Or should you attempt to set an appointment first? While there may be some exceptions to the rule, setting an appointment is generally the wisest move. After all, if the foundation in question has absolutely no interest in meeting you, it's a waste of their time and yours to make the attempt.

Before calling for an appointment, however, it's best to send a personal letter of introduction — one that will set the stage for your upcoming call. Such a letter will make the case for your visit and generally improve your odds of securing an appointment. Additionally, a letter of introduction will add credibility to you and the cause you represent.

Develop a letter of introduction similar to the example at right as a first step in attempting to set an appointment with the new prospect.

Dear <Name>:

I am writing with the hope that you will give me 30 minutes of your time to introduce myself and visit with you about The Boys and Girls Home and its role in our community.

I know that your foundation has a long and successful history in our community and I respect the level of involvement and leadership you have taken in community affairs over the years. The Boys and Girls Home has also had a long history of service to this community, and, for that reason, I believe you and I have some mutual interests.

While it is my genuine hope that you consider a contribution to The Boys and Girls Home, I ask that you meet with me briefly regardless of any decision regarding a gift. I want you to be aware of some of the exciting achievements our organization is making, and ask for your input regarding a future project we are exploring.

I will contact you within the next 10 days to arrange an appointment. Thank you in advance for granting me this opportunity to meet with you.

Sincerely,
<Name>

Introductory Letters That Help Set Appointments

Many development officers would argue that securing that first face-to-face appointment is one of the more crucial steps in the solicitation of a new prospect.

To help ensure a new prospect will say "yes" to your request to meet, begin with a one-page letter that sets the stage for your phone call that will follow.

Your introductory letter should include four key elements:

1. State your objective in the first sentence: to meet with the prospect. Examples of introductory sentences: "You and I have a common friend, [name of friend], who suggested we meet." or "Let me tell you why you and I should meet at a time that's convenient for you."

2. Once the prospect knows you hope to meet with him/her, explain why it's important for you to meet.

3. Next, include a succinct paragraph about your organization's work and how this meeting will allow time to explore common interests.

4. Finally, repeat the fact that you — or another more appropriate individual — will be calling within the next few days to set an appointment.

Be Prepared for That First-time Visit

How prepared are you when calling on a foundation or corporation for the first time? Have you attempted to find out anything about its past giving history? Do you know which organizations the business has supported in recent years? Use this checklist to prepare yourself for first-time calls on foundations or corporations:

- ❑ To what causes has the foundation or corporation contributed in the past years?

- ❑ What are its top funding interests?

- ❑ Who are the decision makers with regard to contributions?

- ❑ When does its fiscal year begin and end?

- ❑ What are the foundations' or corporations' primary products/services?

- ❑ Are gifts made on an ongoing basis or at regular intervals?

- ❑ Does the foundation or corporation have a policy with regard to gifts and sponsorships that is public?

- ❑ What process is followed for submitting gift requests?

- ❑ How is the overall financial well being of the company?

- ❑ Does our organization have any board members, donors or others who also have a relationship with this company?

- ❑ What are the similarities and differences between this company's philosophy and that of your organization?

Tips for Making Introductions to Foundations

Grants consultant Sheryl A. Kaplan (Alhambra, CA) says that while you can initially approach a foundation several ways, it is critical to abide by how a foundation states it wishes to be contacted.

"If you approach a foundation cold, e.g., without a personal contact or relationship, following its guidelines is the single most important thing you can do to start the relationship off on the right foot," Kaplan says.

Foundations may prefer to be contacted by phone or e-mail; by a written letter of inquiry or full grant proposals; or via electronic applications, including letters of inquiry, says Kaplan.

If the foundation requests initial contact be a letter of inquiry of no more than two pages, she says, no amount of calling, submitting a full proposal or sending an e-mail will get you in the door.

"Foundations establish their policies for a reason," the grants consultant says, "and organizations that wish to partner with them to support their programs need to respect those policies."

Face-to-face meetings are another way to contact foundations, says Kaplan. As the foundation becomes inundated with grant requests, program officers have less time for face-to-face meetings, especially those that occur before receiving requests.

While site visits are usually initiated by foundations to give them a first-hand view of the program in action, she says it is appropriate to extend an invitation for a site visit, particularly to local foundations, when you make your request.

Once foundation representatives have your request in hand, they know who you are and have information on the project you seek to fund, seeing the program for themselves can help shape their grant decisions, says Kaplan. A prior relationship or personal contact will give you more flexibility in determining the best way to approach them.

"The foundation will be more receptive to your suggestions for a face-to-face meeting because it knows your organization," she says, "especially if it has been properly cultivated and/or has provided previous support."

Source: Sheryl A. Kaplan, Grants Consultant, Alhambra, CA.
E-mail: sheryl@skaplangrants.com

Connect With Your Nonprofit's Old Timers

You can learn a lot by meeting with and getting to know your organization's old timers — longtime employees who work for you or may have retired, persons having served on your board years ago, even former donors and volunteers who have faded from active involvement.

By identifying and getting to know them you can:

1. Learn more about your organization's history: its programs and services, accomplishments and more — facts that may uncover tools useful to your fundraising efforts.

2. Uncover individual's names who had ties to your organization then but not now.

3. Begin to reconnect and involve these old timers as volunteers and probable donors

Circumstances Determine Best Way to Approach Foundations

 What is the best way to approach a foundation for funding?

"It depends on the foundation. Some you can't get in to see. Others require you to see them face-to-face. My preference would always be to do a face-to-face visit. Ideally, a friend of Seattle Pacific University and the foundation would make an introduction and then an appointment would be made for me to meet with the representative."

— John H. West, Executive Director, Corporate Giving & Foundation Relations, Seattle Pacific University (Seattle, WA)

"It depends on the project and the specific foundation. We have been introduced to foundations in a variety of ways — sometimes by design and sometimes by accident. Faculty members have met program officers at conferences or have been introduced to foundations by colleagues who have received funding. Sometimes program people hear about what we are doing in the national press or are introduced to us by other program officers. Sometimes we simply follow procedures posted on a foundation's website or make a phone call."

— Katie Cervenka, Executive Director, Corporate & Foundation Relations, Rice University (Houston, TX)

Four Tips to Connect With Corporate Decision Makers

Making that first contact with a corporate decision maker can be a challenge. And while a confirmed appointment does not guarantee a gift, the lack of one can certainly diminish likelihood of support. Turn to these techniques to gain entrance to decision makers:

1. If possible, have a mutually respected contact set the appointment and make an introductory visit with you.

2. If making contact on your own, send a brief letter two weeks prior to attempting the appointment. The letter should introduce yourself and explain the purpose of your visit. Call within a few days to set date and time.

3. After contacting the decision maker's assistant, don't simply ask to speak to the decision maker; offer your name first: "Hello, this is Jane White. May I speak with Mr. West?" This gives the impression that you already know Mr. West, improving your likelihood of getting through.

4. If you wrote the decision maker in advance, informing him/her that you would be calling, try this approach: "Hello, this is Jane White. May I please speak to Mr. West? He should be expecting my call."

Three Rules for Meeting With Decision Makers

Before you can make your case, you need to get decision makers to agree to meet with you. Boost your chances for success with these three appointment-setting guidelines:

1. **Should you make the call yourself or have an assistant do it?** Make the call yourself. Your purpose for the call is to develop rapport with the prospect. The call lays the foundation for what will happen at the meeting.

2. **When planning a trip, how hard should you push for a meeting?** If you're traveling to a certain area, identify two sets of dates which you could meet before setting up appointments with prospects. That way, if the prospect says he/she is busy on the first date, you can say, "I also plan to be in your area on (date). Could we meet then?" It will be difficult for the prospect to say "no" twice.

3. **What should you do if you get an answering machine?** If, after several attempts, you still can't connect, leave a message. "This is (name). I'm calling for (institution name). I'm going to be in town on (date) and would like to talk about the exciting things happening at (institution name). Please call me back at (phone number), so we can set a time that works best for you."

Making Presentations to Corporate Gift Committees

The key to making a successful presentation to a corporate gifts committee is developing a strong relationship between your nonprofit and the key decision makers at the corporation. Tailor your presentation to those key decision makers — usually the CEO and/or the head of the corporate giving committee — because if you have them on your side, it doesn't matter who else is involved.

Here are some tips for making presentations to corporate gift committees:

• Align the content of your presentation with the corporation's priorities.

• Let them know beforehand the format that you will use to make your presentation (e.g., Will you use Powerpoint? How much time will you allow for Q&A? Will you provide handouts?).

Corporate Call Tip

■ Even if someone in a company's middle management serves as the point person for initial gift requests, consider relying on a board member or other insider to make a first contact with the company's CEO. That way, when you approach the middle manager to set an appointment or submit a proposal, you can use the CEO's name in your message: "We have chatted with your boss about this project and she asked us to share it with you."

Plan a Tour of Corporate Offices Event

Want to connect with corporate decision makers and raise funds at the same time? Organize a tour of corporate offices in your community.

Base the event on the traditional tour of homes event, applying the same planning procedures for a tour of corporate facilities, especially CEO offices, that the average person rarely sees. Here's how:

1. Identify those corporations and CEO offices you prefer to include on your tour. Prioritize your top choices based on drawing card appeal and decision makers with whom you would most like to build a relationship.

2. Contact the identified CEOs (or other top decision makers) to invite their participation, illustrate benefits and lock in the date of your event. Explain that paying guests will make stops at each corporate tour location to spend about 20 minutes touring lobbies, CEO offices and other points of interest.

3. Involve each corporate participant in planning. Involve each corporate contact in identifying anyone they want to include on the list. Discuss where to focus tour time when each bus load of guests arrive. Iron out details such as decorations, tour procedures, giveaways, refreshments (if offered) and more.

This unique event has a two-fold benefit: you are engaging corporate decision makers in the life of your organization and you can generate special event revenue from those who sign up for the tour.

Corporate Partnership Brochure Lists Involvement Ideas

You have so many options when approaching a corporation for help. If your organization has been able to forge a relationship with a large business, invigorate that relationship by delineating the many ways it can help your major gifts effort.

Develop a marketing piece you can share with your top management contacts that lists the many ways they can help generate more funds for your charity. You can refer to the brochure when meeting with contacts and then leave it with them to consider the possibilities. Below is an example of such a partnership brochure.

WAYS YOU CAN HELP XYZ AGENCY —

Did you know that your business can do even more to help our fundraising efforts? Here's a small sampling of how you help generate gifts that will, in turn, enable us to offer expanded services throughout the community and surrounding region:

Challenge/matching gifts — consider establishing a challenge gift that would match all employees from your corporation who make contributions to our agency.

Sponsorships — we have any number of programs and events that would benefit from sponsorships throughout the year. In addition, your corporation would receive a significant amount of publicity and good will.

Reviewing names of possible employee donors — you no doubt have many employees who are financially capable of helping our organization in significant ways. Would you be willing to discuss who might be worthy of learning more about our agency and its mission? Would you be willing to help introduce us to some of those individuals?

Identifying opportunities for employee involvement with our organization — there are many volunteer opportunities that exist with our agency. Would you consider encouraging employees to take paid time off to assist us?

Assisting us in cultivating relationships with your corporate board members — your willingness to help us forge relationships with any of your board members could result in significant gifts for our agency.

Gifts-in-kind — often times a corporation can provide services or items that significantly help our agency. Examples include printing our brochures in a corporate print shop, providing free manufactured or retail products, etc.

Create a Plan for Securing Corporate Sponsorships

Whether soliciting corporate sponsorships or seeking individual gifts, fundraising is all about relationships, says Todd Stenhouse, president, Stenhouse Strategies (Sacramento, CA) and development officer, National Veterans Foundation (Los Angeles, CA).

Your success will be based on your ability to do six things:

1. **Create a budget and compelling case for support** consistent with your corporate prospects' funding parameters.

2. **Follow 80-20 rule** (80 percent of support will come from 20 percent of donors).

3. **Identify a manageable target group** of companies most interested in your cause or geographically connected to your organization's target population. Learn these companies' culture, missions and objectives. Companies that fit within your sphere are those that will be most approachable with a cold call.

4. **Show companies a return on their investment.** A corporate donor will want to see a return on investment in the form of either service deliverables or public relations, (e.g., a press release, a corporate logo on your website, a corporate naming of an event or award, etc.). Develop a system of metrics for fundraising, as well as monitoring human service programs that will define success.

5. **Have the right person ask.** A peer-to-peer ask is best. With so many nonprofits vying for limited funds from corporations with an interest in their mission, having a staff member or volunteer who can open the door for you can be invaluable.

6. **Say thank you.** Do it three to five times per year, and offer sponsors opportunities to attend events and forums where they see the value of their investment firsthand. Make sure they receive regular press releases, newsletters and other organizational communications to stay informed of the work they make possible.

"An organization is only as good as the number of people it can effectively communicate with," says Stenhouse. "If you can communicate with lots of people, you stand the chance that a sponsor will come to you.... It's important to understand a company's funding protocols, be it by committee, autonomously, voted on, by financial figures supplied by the nonprofit, etc., but sometimes funding comes about just because someone at that company heard or read about you and was compelled to help."

Source: Todd Stenhouse, President, Stenhouse Strategies, Sacramento, CA. Phone (916) 455-6640.
E-mail: todd.stenhouse@comcast.net

Foundation & Corporate Grants: How to Improve Your Funded Grants Batting Average

CULTIVATING FOUNDATION AND CORPORATE RELATIONSHIPS

Cultivating relationships with foundation and corporate funders is both an art and a science. Aim your sights at top decision makers as you move through the funding process. There may be times when you can engage board members and other peers who have connections with these top decision makers.

Build Relationships With Corporate, Foundation Funders

Whether introducing yourself to a foundation program officer or seeking to strengthen a relationship with a corporate giving director, use every means possible to make new introductions and strengthen existing relationships, just as with individual donors.

To create and build relationships with those who can influence your grant request:

- Send an introductory letter that states your intention to arrange an appointment.

- Attend conferences that foundation and corporate gift officers attend.

- Contribute to specialized publications they read.

- Invite them to your events.

- Ask corporate contacts for a tour of their workplace.

- Ask potential funders to speak to your organization or group of nonprofit representatives.

- Join and participate in civic organizations to which they belong.

- Share news clipping on topics in which they are interested.

- Introduce them to individuals they would appreciate knowing.

- Ask them to serve on a committee, task force or your board.

Prepare for a Site Visit

A site visit is a chance for a foundation's program officer to develop a deeper understanding of your organization and your proposal, says Scott Sheldon, associate vice president for annual giving, Scottsdale Healthcare Foundation (Scottsdale AZ).

"During the site visit, the program officer will get a chance to meet you face-to-face and discuss specific details about your organization's programs, staffing, financial situation, board of directors, etc.," Sheldon says. "A site visit is an opportunity for you to bring your organization to life in a way that just doesn't happen by reading a proposal."

He shares his advice for preparing for and making the most of a site visit:

- **Decide who and how many people from your organization will be present at the site visit.** Too many people can be overwhelming and make the process take longer than necessary. Choose no more than three or four people, including the staff leader (e.g., the executive director, president, or CEO); someone who can answer financial questions; and, depending on

your proposal: director of the program you are seeking to fund; development director or other person who wrote the grant; president or other board of directors member; or recipient of services. The program officer may bring another program officer, staff member, or advisory committee member along, but he or she will let you know that prior to the visit.

- **Re-read your proposal and have it available during the site visit.**

- **Put yourself in the program officer's shoes, imagining what you would ask if just learning about your organization.** Program officers may forward a list of questions in advance, but additional questions may arise during the visit. Be ready to answer them. If you don't have requested information available, track it down and get it to the program officer as soon as you can.

Source: Scott Sheldon, associate vice president, annual giving, Scottsdale Healthcare Foundaiton, Scottsdale, AZ.
Phone (877) 898-6569.

Aim Your Sights at Upper Management

We're often so focused on the company CEO that we lose sight of the massive giving potential of those persons who surround a company's top official.

Individuals within upper management should be considered viable prospects for several reasons: many receive high salaries, have contacts with other higher ups and possess the ability to get things done and to influence company decisions.

Employ these strategies to involve and build relationships with persons in upper management positions:

✓ Assign someone to research your community directory and other resources, adding names and addresses of corporate vice presidents and company officers to your mailing list.

✓ Explore ways to cultivate and involve spouses of upper management personnel.

✓ Identify corporate executives who have an existing relationship with your organization. Meet with them one on one to formulate cultivation strategies aimed at upper level professionals within their respective companies.

✓ Establish a business and corporate advisory committee made up of people who are already committed to your nonprofit. Meet regularly with the group to develop cultivation strategies and programs.

✓ Establish a corporate executive of the month award (or multiple awards in different categories) that recognizes professionals for achievement in some area (e.g., civic involvement, professional achievement). Include all past award recipients in an ongoing society that meets at least yearly.

✓ Identify 10 key issues facing your organization's future that corporate involvement could impact positively. Use the challenges as a way to involve executives in your agency over a multi-year period.

✓ Form a corporate partners program with accompanying benefits for corporate executives who join or contribute. Provide benefits offering value to the corporate executive: discounts at restaurants, golf outings, tickets to events, receptions conducive to networking, etc.

✓ As part of a yearlong communications plan, incorporate profiles of key executives into your regularly published newsletter or magazine. Develop feature stories and submit news releases including upper management individuals who are engaged in your organization as volunteers, board members or donors.

Cultivate Support Through Corporate Giving Officers

It's a long-standing fundraising axiom: People give to people.

That's why it's helpful to meet and get to know those professionals in the corporate world who are charged with corporate contributions.

Here are some ways to make contact and cultivate support:

• Determine which of your institution's vendors do business with the companies in mind. They may help in making an introduction or even soliciting a gift.

• Establish rapport with consultants who give advice to corporate giving officers.

• Create a quarterly letter that updates your mailing list's contributions committees.

• Identify groups/clubs that corporate employees belong to and get involved.

• When meeting with corporate giving officers, ask them for names of their counterparts at other companies.

• Share names of corporate contributions committee members with your board. Ask for their help in opening doors.

Create a Traveling Ambassador Corps to Assist in Cultivation

Do you have a board member making a business trip to the East or West Coast? What about that retired board member who vacations in Florida each winter? Turn these and other close friends of your organization into traveling ambassadors by involving them in cultivating major gift prospects who live at or near their travel destinations.

These traveling ambassadors can help do their part to enhance the image and work of your organization throughout the nation.

Use an anticipated trips form such as the one at right to pinpoint opportunities to involve persons in identifying, cultivating, researching and even soliciting gifts on your behalf.

In their travels, these persons could assist you by:

- Hosting a reception.
- Conducting prospect research on individuals, businesses or foundations in that region.
- Making introductory calls.
- Delivering a message of thanks for past support.
- Hand-delivering a proposal.
- Seeking donated items for events.

Rather than sending or e-mailing forms, distribute them at board meetings to explain how helpful involvement can be with these out-of-town prospects. Share the forms selectively on a one-to-one basis with others who travel in affluent circles.

When you receive a completed form, identify appropriate fund development activities and discuss them with the person submitting the form before departure.

Sharing this form will have multiple benefits:

- Completed forms help keep your office posted on the schedules of board members and others.
- By involving these persons in the fund development process, you are also engaging them — helping them more fully own the role of major gifts at your institution.
- Their involvement will help realize cultivation, research and solicitation that otherwise might not have been accomplished.

RANDOM UNIVERSITY
Anticipated Trips Form

This form is for board members and other Random University insiders who wish to serve as ambassadors during their business and leisure travels.

When a trip is planned, simply complete this form and turn in to the Institutional Advancement Office. A development officer will contact you to go over possible ways in which you could assist in making contacts with individuals. Thank you!

Name _____

Trip Destination _____

❏ Business   ❏ Pleasure

Trip Arrival Date_____ Departure Date_____

Where You Can Be Reached During Trip:

Address _____ E-mail _____

Phone (_____) _____ Fax_____

Examples of Ambassador activities with which you might assist:

❏ Introductory visits:
  ❏ With individuals
  ❏ With business representatives
  ❏ With foundations

❏ Friendship-building activities
❏ Distributing literature about Random University
❏ Hosting a reception
❏ Identifying potential contributors
❏ Telephoning friends/donors of the university
❏ Soliciting a gift
❏ Delivering a proposal
❏ Securing donated items for our annual gala
❏ Other (Please describe.) _____
_____
_____
_____
_____
_____

Work at Cultivating Corporate Relationships

To capture the attention of corporate decision makers, establish a procedure that maximizes introductions and helps contacts learn more about your organization and its worthiness for major gift support.

Follow these basic steps to help formulate a partnership-building procedure:

1. **Identify the key decision makers in your service area.** Make a list with contact information and attempt to prioritize your list according to: 1) gift capability and 2) proclivity to give (based on past giving to and involvement with your charity).

2. **Systematically begin setting one appointment each week to meet with a decision maker on your list.** Use the initial meeting to educate the individual about your mission and begin to explore how you might work together on any number of projects: employee mentors; internships; employee volunteering at your organization; company sponsored event or program; employee-giving campaign to your charity; etc. End the meeting by agreeing to another on-site meeting time where you can provide a personal tour of your facilities.

3. **Meet on your turf and provide an in-depth tour for each decision maker.** Tailor each tour to what you perceive to be key interests of each decision maker.

4. **Meet a third time with each decision maker to formalize partnership plans.** Offer a written proposal that outlines what you have in mind and requires the signature of the decision maker.

> ### Cultivation Tip
>
> When you learn of a corporation's plans to have a public reception or open house, contact its decision-maker about showcasing your nonprofit as part of the festivities.
>
> What's in it for the corporation? The chance to look like a conscientious corporate citizen and boost event attendance.

Turn Corporate Prospects Into Corporate Sponsors

Obtaining corporate sponsorship can be a financially sound way of supporting your next fundraising event. However, securing corporate sponsors — particularly in today's economic climate — can prove challenging. To win over your corporate sponsors:

❑ Create a corporate sponsorship brochure that outlines details of your event and clearly states where sponsorship dollars will be placed.

❑ Don't rely solely on mailers to obtain corporate sponsors. Would you give $10,000 to someone you'd never met? Of course not. Meet face-to-face with sponsors. Prepare a presentation that concisely details your fundraising efforts and gives insight to how sponsorship will assist not only your event, but your organization as a whole.

❑ Supply the potential sponsor with the history of your organization.

❑ Provide quantifiable numbers from previous years' events and how the funds raised were utilized.

❑ Show how sponsorship will benefit their company. Clearly relay details as to where the sponsor logos will appear, including logo prominence and number of times the logo will be seen in your community. Explain what each event participant and attendee receives such as giveaways — backed by corporate sponsorship dollars and displayed with the company's logo.

❑ Describe available sponsorship levels and benefits of each. Be specific about your event marketing plan, ad placement and how you'll maximize publicity to promote the event and spotlight its sponsors.

❑ Ask the corporation to not only front the cash, but to participate in your special event. During the sponsorship meeting, encourage participation of the company's employees in the event as a team or individually.

> ### Attract More Corporate Gifts
>
> Need more pull in attracting gifts from corporations? Here's an idea: Any corporation that makes an investment of $10,000 or more per year gets to select one representative to serve on your board or advisory council.

❑ Provide contact information for later questions and set up a follow-up meeting or time to contact the potential sponsor to confirm participation level.

❑ Send a thank-you note to those included in the meeting. A handwritten, heartfelt note will make a positive lasting impression every time.

Foundation & Corporate Grants: How to Improve Your Funded Grants Batting Average

What goes into drafting a winning grant proposal? What key points should your proposal address? How long should it be? How can you make a compelling request for support? What should your proposal look like? How can you best demonstrate the impact a grant will have on your organization and those you serve? This chapter will address these and other important questions.

How to Develop Your Master Grant Proposal

Your master grant proposal should have certain elements that reflect basic journalism principles – the who, what, when, where, why, and how of your project, says Alice L. Ferris, ACFRE, a partner with GoalBusters Consulting, LLC (Flagstaff, AZ), because they are all things you will need to think about when you're starting to develop your master proposal or foundation prospect list.

"The who, what and where are the broad overview questions," says Ferris. "Usually if I can get down to the who, what and where in broad strokes with program staff and I don't think I have a funder that it will match up to right away, that's my mini prospectus which goes into a portfolio of all the major projects that I would be looking for funding for."

Who — the people who will be involved in the direct administration of the program.

"You can allocate a portion of your CEO or grant professional/development person's time to this project as long as they really will be spending that amount of time on it," she says. "Don't pick a random percentage. Come up with an actual dollar amount and base it on your wage." Also, she says, collect the curriculum vitae/resumes of these people early on as opposed to later when you might be on deadline and have to chase down somebody for it."

What — the details of the actual project, how it was conceived, what need created this program, what your core messages are, what the project will do and what your goals are.

Where — whether the project will be conducted at one site or multiple sites and the demographics of each location.

When — the start date of the project, how long it will take and whether it is for a limited time or ongoing.

"If you have a project that won't start for a year, that's perfect," she says. "You want about a year to find the funding needed for the project. Ideally, you want a start date six months to a year in the future."

Why — the detailed needs assessment for a project or reason for pushing it further though the process.

"If you are a social service agency, for example, it's where you will look at how many of your population are potential clients for this program, why you need the program, what other agencies are already potentially providing services to that audience, what other resources are available in the community and where the gap is. Also, ask yourself whose lives will be improved and what will be the end result of one year, two years and three years of the program to start to get into the story of your program," she says.

How — the actual action steps, timeline, budget and resources for your program.

"Look at the end point of the grant period and work backwards to make sure you'll have time to finish everything you want to finish," says Ferris. "Put a specific name or title next to each action step. Make sure you have someone specifically assigned to each one of those action steps to make sure there is someone who will do it."

Source: Alice L. Ferris, ACFRE, Partner, GoalBusters Consulting, LLC, Flagstaff, AZ. Phone (888) 883-2690. E-mail: alice.ferris@goalbusters.net

---

Tips for Winning Proposals

- Proposals that most often get funded offer solutions to an existing problem and list measurable outcomes of the project's success.

- The proposal should include a detailed budget of how the grant will be used throughout the duration of the project.

Grant Writing Tip

Writing a grant request? Keep in mind that when reviewing grant proposals, funders want to see quantifiable facts supported by anecdotes, not anecdotes supported by facts.

Following a Proposal Preparation Process Can Be Rewarding

While many foundations provide very clear-cut guidelines and procedures for submitting grant requests, others are more ambiguous, sometimes by design.

In situations where you're left more on your own to set the stage for funding, it helps to have an outline from which to craft both your proposal and its accompanying cover letter (see box, below).

It's obviously important that your request for funds be tailored to a specific project and address the interests of the foundation recipient. However, having an outline from which to proceed will help to create organization and ensure that key components are being fully addressed.

In developing a cover letter, try to keep it to a page if possible and have it come from your organization's CEO. Or, if you have another connection such as a board member whose name and/or position would be recognized by foundation officials, have that person sign it.

Here's another tip: Find out which organizations the foundation in question has funded in recent years, then contact two or three of them and ask if they would be willing to share a copy of their request or at least discuss what went into their proposals. You may find these people open to an exchange of ideas and methods on how to successfully approach foundations.

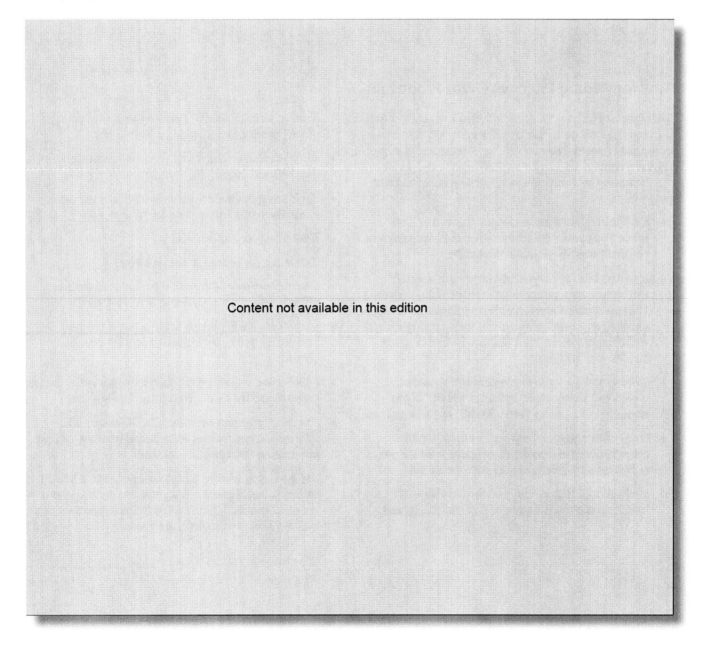

Content not available in this edition

Advice for New Grant Writers

For those of you new to grant writing, Barbara Kellogg, associate director of planning and development, North Iowa Community Action Organization (Mason City, IA), recommends the following:

- **Read and review grant applications.** "I've been writing grants for 26 years and feel strongly that the opportunity to read and review other people's grant applications early on in my career was one of the most important steps in increasing my own grant writing skills," Kellogg says.

- **Attend workshops.** Some may be more beneficial than others, but she says she always gained something — a new skill, idea or contact.

- **Network.** Kellogg says she meets regularly with two groups of peers and calls networking "an invaluable resource to every grant writer."

Source: Barbara Kellogg, Associate Director of Planning and Development, North Iowa Community Action Organization, Mason City, IA. Phone (641) 423-8993. E-mail: bkellogg@nicao-online.org. Website: www.nicao-online.org

Tips for Writing Effective Grant Proposals

Let's assume you know your organization's target for a funding proposal, how much you are asking for, and the purpose of the grant request. Now it's time to sit down and start writing the proposal.

Following are practical tips for writing effective grant proposals:

- Keep the request short, no longer than two or three pages. Most prospects are overwhelmed with paper and you don't want to get lost in the shuffle.

- If writing to a foundation, talk in terms of a gift. If writing to a corporation, write in terms of an investment. The two organizational types have different mind-sets; foundations are in the business of giving money away while corporations try to make money. Use language that fits your prospect.

- Make your request's verb tense positive instead of conditional. For example, instead of writing "If you would consider," write "Your gift will" or "Your gift can."

- Study other agencies the group has funded. Call colleagues who obtained gifts or grants from the group to find out why their proposals were successful.

- Study all materials available on the foundation or funding group to get a sense of their philosophy and general overall interests. Focus on aspects of your project that are in tune with that philosophy.

- Write in clear, concise form. Avoid burdensome language and jargon.

- Short sentences make your proposal easier to read. Break the subject matter into bite-size pieces.

- Underline your request.

- Talk about opportunities, not problems.

- Cite the relevance of the gift to the donor. Show how the gift is as important to the donor as it is to the recipient.

- Credentials are important. Make sure the organization knows your group is qualified to do what you are proposing.

- Follow grant application directions provided by the funding organization. Their requirements are usually clear.

- Proofread your proposal carefully. Make sure all information presented is accurate and relevant, and that information throughout corresponds.

- Say thank you whether or not your proposal is funded. If such acknowledgment is not given, the donor group may not be interested in funding you the next time a request is made. Handwritten notes are good.

How to Make Your Next Major Gifts Proposal Compelling

Lydia Palmer, director of development communications, Rochester Institute of Technology (Rochester, NY), says not just anyone can write a compelling major gifts proposal.

"It's been my experience that few people have the skill set of sales/development knowledge, writing ability, project management skills and creative layout ability to construct a good proposal," says Palmer. "Even people I've met who have spent their lives writing grant proposals or working in major gifts fund raising, when asked to write a major gift proposal, turn it into a torturous effort."

Palmer shares her experience and advice for writing a major gifts proposal.

What needs to occur before you sit down to write a proposal?

"A major gift proposal should be a written outline of what has been discussed with a prospect and put forward in a formal request. Major gift proposals should not be used as an opportunity to float options to prospects to see if anything sticks."

She says there are three steps that need addressing prior to drafting a proposal:

- The development officer and/or volunteer should meet with the prospect and establish that the organization is going to make a formal request for a significant gift.
- Identify the real giving range for the prospect.
- Determine the broad area of donor interest.

Explain the writing process you follow when creating a proposal.

"I write it as a prospect would read it. The introduction of and the reason for what we're asking comes first, then small sections for details. If a point has a lot of support information, I try to push those things to appendices," says Palmer.

"I usually work with a framework in my head. Hopefully, the proposal isn't so complicated it requires a full-fledged outline. If it's that complicated, consider simplifying the ask. You can make your case succinct and clearly or you can't."

How do you make the proposal compelling?

"The proposal isn't going to convince anyone to make a major gift — it's the discussions, tours, personal testimonies, etc. The proposal just solidifies what the prospect should already know about your organization."

What is the rule of thumb regarding the length of a proposal?

"Know your prospect. Some prospects like to be loaded with details, charts, layouts, case studies, bios and profiles, etc. Others don't want to know those details — they want to know how you're going to use the money and how you'll know you've been successful."

Source: Lydia Palmer, Director, Development Communication, Rochester Institute of Technology, Rochester, NY. Phone (585) 475-6289. E-mail: lspdar@rit.edu

How to Incorporate Persuasive Text Into Proposals

The three critical steps to securing funding from a corporation or foundation: 1) Make your proposal stand out, 2) engage the reader's interest and 3) build a compelling case.

All three steps can be achieved through use of persuasive text, says Jessica Indrigo, senior associate director of corporate and foundation relations, Washington University School of Medicine (St. Louis, MO).

"While the beneficial effects of a proposed project may be obvious to stakeholders," Indrigo says, "they may not be clear to the funder who has read multiple proposals for seemingly similar projects."

To incorporate persuasive text into your proposals, Indrigo advises:

- Define the solution by listing the proposed project's measurable goals and describing its quantitative impact.

- Document the need for the proposed project with facts, preferably from objective sources. "A string of adjectives is likely to be dismissed as empty hype," she says.

- Demonstrate quality of leadership, unique resources and a history of relevant accomplishments — elements that distinguish an organization from its peers.

- Convey passion for the proposed project using strong declarative verbs and an active voice.

Source: Jessica Indrigo, Senior Associate Director of Corporate and Foundation Relations, Washington University School of Medicine, St. Louis, MO. Phone (314) 935-9687. E-mail: indrigoj@wustl.edu

What Should a Grant Proposal Look Like?

Most foundations provide very strict guidelines for submitting grant proposals, but what should you do if they don't?

Cheryl A. Clarke, fundraising consultant and trainer (Mill Valley, CA), says when a foundation doesn't provide any guidelines, organizations should follow this framework for organizing a grant proposal:

- **Intro/Summary**
- **Agency History/Mission**
- **Need or Problem Being Addressed** (includes defining the constituency being served and where)
- **Outcomes** (proposed results or changes that will occur)
- **Methods** (or project description — what you are actually going to do)
- **Evaluation** (how you plan to assess the outcomes and methods)
- **Future Funding** (how you plan to fund the program in the future)
- **Conclusion**

"Proposals should make a persuasive case," says Clarke. "I strongly believe in telling a good story to the funder, one that will inform as well as persuade."

Clarke says her typical proposal narrative is three to five pages.

Source: Cheryl A. Clarke, Fundraising Consultant and Trainer, Mill Valley, CA. Phone (415) 388-9126. E-mail: cheryl@cherylaclarke.com

---

Grant Proposal Writing Dos and Don'ts

Fundraising consultant and trainer Cheryl A. Clarke (Mill Valley, CA) shares these dos and don'ts for writing grant proposals:

- Follow guidelines to the letter.
- Proofread, proofread, proofread, then get someone else to proofread.
- Never assume the reader knows about your community's need, your constituency or your agency. Be thorough and tell them.
- Do not exaggerate.
- Write in an energetic style using present tense and an active voice.
- Use simple, clear language.
- Remember you are writing to and for a real person.
- Cite primary sources when including data.
- Make all information as clear and obvious as possible.

Demonstrate the Cumulative Impact of a Gift

As you approach the point of solicitation, it's helpful to show a prospect how a particular gift will impact your organization and those you serve over time. This is particularly useful with certain types of major gifts (e.g., endowment, programming and personnel).

You can illustrate the long-term impact of a gift as a portion of your written proposal or it can be shared as a stand-alone document. Referred to as a gift impact summary, this can also be used as a tool to help negotiate the exact terms of a particular gift. In the case of an endowed scholarship, for instance, the number of students to receive awards, the individual award amounts and other details can be finalized by using the summary as a starting point.

The gift impact summary also helps ensure that both the donor and charity are on the same page with regard to details surrounding the actual gift (e.g., payment schedule, when the fund begins) and its eventual use (e.g., who benefits, how many, etc).

Two generic examples (shown at right) help illustrate the most basic types of information you might wish to include in your gift impact summary. Your actual summary would no doubt be lengthier and include more detailed information.

Examples of Gift Impact Summaries

Named Endowed Scholarship
Gift Amount: $100,000 Anticipated Yearly Award (five percent): $5,000

Use of Gift: To provide annual scholarship awards to financially deserving women majoring in math or science.

Five-Year Results:
25 Cumulative Scholarship Awards at $1,000 each.

10-Year Results:
50 Cumulative Scholarship Awards at $1,000 each.

Domestic Violence Endowment
Gift Amount: $250,000 Anticipated Yearly Funds (five percent): $12,500

Use of Gift: To provide career assistance and job placement opportunities for adults seeking shelter at the agency by underwriting, in part, an employee position responsible for assisting clients with career development and job placement opportunities.

Five-Year Results:
Based on past occupancy rates, career and job assistance will have been available to more than 1,000 deserving clients.

10-Year Results:
Based on past occupancy rates, career and job assistance will have been available to more than 2,000 deserving clients.

Include an Executive Summary With All Proposals

Do you follow a standard outline when crafting major gift proposals? Whether you do or not, make a point to include an executive summary at the beginning of your written document. Why? Two reasons:

1. A properly written proposal summary will tempt the potential donor to read on. As you draft the summary, view it through the eyes of the would-be donor. In 200 words or less, what can you say that will captivate the reader? Obviously, the proposed name of the fund or building project will draw attention. The way you describe the impact of the donor's gift may also come into play. If the donor has an obvious interest in the future growth of a proposed endowment fund or the annual interest from it, for instance, you may want to devote more wordage to the way the gift will be invested and how it relates to your overall endowment.

2. Summaries will also help to ensure readers see the document's big picture if they choose not to read anything more. Knowing this, be sure to include in the summary the ask amount, what the realization of that gift would accomplish, and the benefits to the donor for making that gift a reality. Do not include the payout period for your request; that's an item that can be negotiated as the gift is finalized.

Sample executive summary for a proposed endowment gift.

Content not available in this edition

Write More Grant Proposals

While grant writers often rely on others' input as they strive to churn out requests, it's important to keep the process moving to maximize the number of submitted proposals. Take these steps to move the grant-writing process along:

1. **Agree on substance before polishing the words.** Don't get too absorbed in writing until you're sure of a proposal's substance. First meet with those whose input is needed to determine direction and draft an outline encompassing their thoughts.

2. **Divide the proposal into components that can be more easily managed.** If writing out the budget prior to the project description makes sense, then by all means, do so.

3. **Set deadlines.** Just as important as breaking down grant-writing process components, assign deadlines to each component. Inform all involved to avoid committee delays.

4. **Set aside writing time religiously.** Determine what time of day you do your best writing and maintain a closed door policy at that time. Colleagues will soon learn to set appointments that don't interfere with your concentration time.

5. **Reward yourself for staying on track.** Whether you do 10 or 100 proposals a year, recognize your accomplishments and reward yourself. Doing so gives you a breather between proposals and incentive to stay on task.

When It Makes Sense to Outsource Grant Writing

Outsourcing grant writing makes sense for nonprofits without the time or expertise to do the job consistently and with quality, says John Glenn, executive vice president, director of communications, The Steier Group (Omaha, NE).

"Grant writing is a very special skill," he says. "It is very specific, artful and concise. To have someone writing grants part-time or as a secondary endeavor usually doesn't produce the result a nonprofit wants or needs."

Many firms, like The Steier Group, offer full- or part-time grant writing services. They usually charge a monthly fee, says Glenn, which includes the expectation that the grant writer will write and submit a certain number of grants within that time.

Nonprofits outsource their grant writing for several reasons, he says, including:

- **The ability to work with a full-time grant writer** who has honed his or her grant writing and research skills to help identify what foundations match a particular nonprofit's project.

- **Cost savings.** Hiring a full-time in-house grant writer involves additional costs such as employee benefits and equipment. Contracting grant-writing services with a firm maximizes a grant writer's time and expertise, which also saves money.

- **Access to valuable search engines** that allow them to broaden the net for possible funders.

- **Time savings.** Because many nonprofits cannot afford a full-time grant writer, the job falls to the person who is also working on the annual fund and event planning. Outsourcing grant writing allows that person more time to work on those tasks.

"It's really important to make sure your nonprofit is a true partner with your outside grant writer," says Glenn. "A relationship needs to be built up between your nonprofit and the grant writer to ensure that he or she can articulate your vision and mission to a funder with passion."

Your grant writer should be willing to take the time to get a full understanding of your nonprofit's mission and vision, and how you live it, he says, adding that you should not only have the ability to review the proposal before it is submitted, but be part of the process of creating the proposal.

Source: John Glenn, Executive Vice President, Director of Communications, The Steier Group, Omaha, NE. Phone (866) 391-3244. E-mail: jglenn@steiergroup.com

Take Steps to Finalize Written Proposals

Before submitting a written proposal to a foundation or corporation, ask a colleague not directly involved with the project to review it looking for:

✓ Mistakes of grammar, punctuation and spelling.

✓ Inconsistencies in logic.

✓ Unjustified budget items.

✓ Undefined or confusing terms.

✓ Unsupported arguments, unfounded assumptions or weak documentation.

✓ Ways to make messages more compelling.

Add Clout to Proposals

Before delivering a written proposal to an individual or business, have a place for your organization's CEO to sign and date it. Having your organization's chief officer sign off on the proposal adds strength and credibility to it.

Writing Tip: Read it Out Loud

The best way to ensure what you've written is easy to read, clear and understandable is to read it out loud.

If you find yourself tripping over words as you read them or stopping and asking, "What did that say?" — it's time for a rewrite.

Foundation & Corporate Grants: How to Improve Your Funded Grants Batting Average

Just because you're successful in securing a grant doesn't mean the work is over. In fact, in many ways the work is just getting underway. The fact that you are accepting a grant obligates your organization to adhere to and fulfill what you promised the grant would accomplish. It's called stewardship. And equally important, there are steps you should take even when your grant request is rejected.

Advice on Publicizing Foundation Grants

Q. *"How do you determine whether to publicize a foundation grant, to what degree, and which types of publicity to use? Can you share any cautionary notes regarding publicizing a foundation grant?"*

"All organizations should eventually develop donor recognition policies regarding how they recognize gifts from all donors, including corporations and foundations. If clear policies are in place and already approved by the organization's leadership, then it will be easier to make decisions when individual issues come up. Such policies also help organizations set clear expectations with funders ahead of time as to the nature of recognition to be expected for a particular size of gift.

"For example, one organization may decide that they will issue a press release for any foundation gift over $10,000, while for another organization, the policy might be to publicize any gift whatever the size. Your policies should include what size and type of gift merit a permanent sign in a facility, what size such plaques should be and of what material. The policies should address naming rights: what size gift is required to name something after the funder and how to determine when something needs to be unnamed if the funder's name later becomes a liability rather than an asset (think of Enron).

"Press releases, with photos if applicable, are probably the most common ways to publicize foundation gifts. However, other common strategies include newsletter articles, profiles on the recipient's website, coverage in the annual report or glossy magazine put out by the recipient or even press conferences for really extraordinary gifts. A sign or plaque honoring the foundation for its gift is also common.

"In most cases, a foundation gift is publicized when it is received. There are a few exceptions. Sometimes you coordinate the photo op of the foundation officer presenting the gift with a special event or schedule it when board members can be present. Challenge grants require extensive publicity — that's their purpose. Thus, the publicity begins as soon as the challenge is issued and the challenge is publicized as extensively as possible in order to generate gifts in response. Then, of course, the gift is publicized once again when the challenge has been successfully met and the money is actually received from the foundation.

"Be sure to always honor the foundation's wishes regarding publicity unless there is a legal or ethical reason not to. When creating a sign to honor the foundation, make sure to let the foundation approve the text and formatting of the sign before having it made. Many foundations either provide the content or require that they be allowed to approve the content of press releases about their gift before the release goes out. Others request that you insert a statement that describes their foundation in a particular way. A very few wish to remain anonymous and you should honor this request as well. It is worth a call to the foundation to clarify exactly how far they wish to carry their anonymity. In other words, may you publicize the gift and its purpose while stating that the donor was anonymous? Or will they insist on no publicity at all?

"Consider publicity of foundation gifts an important part of saying 'thank you' to the funder. Most foundations and corporations are very interested in how much publicity they will receive for making their gift. For the exceptions who wish to remain anonymous, honoring their wishes is the best 'thank you' you can give them."

— *Cheryl Kester, partner, Thomas-Forbes & Kester Grants Consulting (Fayetteville, AR)*

Follow Grant Publication Policy

Q. We do not currently have a clear policy on publicizing corporate, foundation or government grants. Should we publicize all grants? Should we get permission from the funder before publicizing a grant? What are the advantages of publicizing a grant?

"From the community foundation perspective, we love to have grantees publicize their efforts. To that end, we send sample press releases with our grant award letters. We've even added language in our contract that asks for a copy of press releases. We don't have to vet them, but we're happy to offer a quote raving about the institution/project for inclusion. As anything related to grants, I think publicity falls under what would the donor want, followed by what does your organization want. Anonymous gifts can still be trumpeted. Also, in terms of garnering press, it's all about the project story, not the gift story. Unless the gift is so large or unique that the paper thinks it's worth talking about, you've got to use the gift as an entree into a story about the impact of your project."

— *Tom Linfield, Vice President, Grantmaking and Community Initiatives, Madison Community Foundation (Madison, WI)*

"At Hartwick we publicize all grants unless publicity is specifically prohibited by the funder. All press releases are approved by the foundation or grantmaking agency.... Good PR can only enhance our reputation locally, regionally and nationally."

— *Margaret Arthurs, Director of Corporate, Foundation and Government Relations, Hartwick College (Oneonta, NY)*

"Gifts are almost always good publicity. I'd suggest contacting the foundation/corporation before publicizing the gift for two reasons: 1) They may not want the gift publicized, especially in the current economic climate. For example, a corporation that received bailout money of some sort might not want their philanthropy publicized; 2) You want their boilerplate language and quotes for your release, as well as any logos. Remember, the publicity is not just for your institution, but theirs as well. Helping build their reputation also helps build your relationship with the organization."

— *Kelley Skillin, Director of Special Projects for the Office of the Provost, Wayne State University (Detroit, MI)*

Tips for Developing Grantee Reports

Most foundations require grantees to report on the progress of the grant they have funded, usually every six to 12 months after the grant has been awarded, and then at the end of the grant period. While most foundations provide guidelines for creating these grantee reports, doing so can still be daunting for new grantees.

Here's advice officials with the University of Hawaii Foundation give to aid faculty members in writing grantee reports:

- Begin by listing the organization and project information. Include grant ID numbers; organization's name and address; name and title of person preparing the report; project name; time frame covered in the report and time frame of the project.

- Provide a brief description of the accomplishments, challenges and lessons learned related to the project during the reporting period.

- Use the goals, objectives and outcomes outlined in the original proposal as a guide for the report. Indicate the impact of funding.

- Keep the report brief — less than five pages.

- Provide a complete accounting of the grant and total project expenses in the financial section of the report. If the expenses are not aligned with the original proposal budget submitted, include a description and explanation of the changes.

When You're Declined By a Foundation

To improve your odds for future grants, find out what needs to be corrected when your request for funding has been denied:

1. Thank foundation personnel for having given your request full consideration.

2. Find out where you missed the mark. If you can't get the reasons in writing, make a point to meet with the appropriate foundation staff member and get his/her assessment.

Appropriate Gifts to Say Thanks to Foundations

 We would like to thank our foundation donors for their recent grants to our organization. What type of gifts do foundations prefer to receive?

"Frequently, development-oriented people react to foundation giving with an individual giving mindset rather than a foundation mindset. Unless it's a small family foundation — which is often just a vehicle by which individuals are doing their personal giving — this doesn't work. At my first foundation relations job, as early as the interview process it became apparent to me that the top folks in development did not understand that foundation giving works differently than individual giving. It's important to match the mode of thanks to the motivation for giving — individuals like personal recognition, corporations like visibility and foundations like knowing they've done good. A sincere letter of thanks and a press release, which you have cleared with the foundation, usually takes care of that!"

— Deborah S. Koch, Director of Grants,
Springfield Technical Community College (Springfield, MA)

"It depends on the foundation, of course. Recently, we did something that worked well for one of our major foundation donors. The foundation had been giving to us a yearly grant to be used for scholarships for 28 years. We contacted all of the previous student recipients and asked them to write a letter of thanks to the foundation. About 20 students responded with wonderful letters of where they are now and how the scholarship helped them achieve their goals. We then put the letters together with a recent picture and their yearbook picture in a Snapfish photobook. The foundation loved it! We also kept a copy for the development office and use it when we meet with prospective donors to show the impact of scholarships on our students."

— Suzanne Libenson, Director of Foundation Relations and
Government Funding, Holy Family University (Philadelphia, PA)

"Because we're a small, private institution, we try not to be too extravagant when it comes to donor recognition. All donors, including foundation donors, receive an official thank-you letter from our president. I also handwrite a note to our foundation donors and call them if I happen to know someone at the foundation. If the grant is for student scholarships, students will also write thank-you letters to the foundation. Foundation donors are also recognized on our outdoor donor recognition wall, on giving society plaques in our administration building and in the college's online annual Honor Roll of Donors."

— Cindy C. Godwin, Director of Development,
Meredith College (Raleigh, NC)

Foundation & Corporate Grants: How to Improve Your Funded Grants Batting Average

IDEAS, STRATEGIES WORTH CONSIDERING

Following are some useful ideas — as well as useful references — you should consider as you work to build and improve your foundation/corporate giving program.

Foundation Challenge Gifts Help Carry Momentum

Once you have at least 50 percent of your campaign goal in hand and you have announced the public phase of your campaign, consider going after challenge grants from foundations (e.g., Kresge Foundation) to help carry you through to the end.

A challenge grant from a foundation has threefold benefits:

1. Putting your foundation proposal in the form of a challenge may be what it takes to secure the foundation grant.

2. Doing so can help motivate new pledges throughout your campaign's public phase.

3. In addition to new pledges, you may be able to make return visits to those who made lead gifts, inviting them to up their pledges in response to the challenge grant.

What It Takes to Land a Kresge Challenge

In 2008, Florida Southern College (Lakeland, FL) received a $600,000 Kresge Foundation Capital Challenge Grant to help with the construction of a new academic building for the study of literature and languages.

The challenge grant was also given to encourage broad-based participation from the college's alumni and friends. The terms of the grant required the college to raise the project balance of $1.97 million within 18 months.

"We met our goal five months ahead of schedule," says Lee Mayhall, vice president for college relations.

Securing a Kresge Foundation Challenge Grant is a lengthy process, she says, and requires a major commitment on the part of the institution's leadership. "Every one of our trustees made a financial commitment to the project prior to the submission of our proposal, with the president, trustees and volunteers participating in gift solicitations."

Prior to submission of their proposal, the college's president visited the foundation to discuss their challenge grant campaign strategy, she says.

A strong campaign was also important to the success of the proposal. "The foundation assumes your project is worthy — they want to see a solid plan for achieving the balance of the project goal," says Mayhall.

The college's plan included communications to stakeholders and staff, and volunteer involvement in the solicitation of top prospects (e.g., trustees, corporations and foundations, and individuals). "It also included a well-organized program of soliciting broad-based support from alumni, parents and faculty/staff," she says.

Once funded, it is crucial to stay in regular communication with your grants compliance officer, who wants your project to succeed, says Mayhall. The Kresge Foundation required periodic financial and construction progress reports.

She shares this advice for other fundraisers seeking to land a Kresge Challenge:

- Make sure that your project and fundraising timetable fit the foundation's guidelines. Ensure institutional commitment from the president, trustees, major gifts and annual fund staff, and your vice president for facilities. Securing and meeting a Kresge Foundation Challenge Grant can take more than two years.

- Maintain frequent communication with the foundation during the challenge grant phase.

Source: Lee Mayhall, Vice President for College Relations, Development Office, Florida Southern College, Lakeland, FL. Phone (863) 680-4986. E-mail: lmayhall@flsouthern.edu

Negotiating a Challenge Grant

A donor approaches you about making a large challenge grant, but you've never done one. You wonder: Will the challenge grant be worth the work involved?

Susan D. Smith, consultant, Susan D. Smith Consultant in Philanthropy (Barneveld, NY), says challenge grants are a great opportunity for attracting new and/or increased gifts, and, with good planning, can also provide the opportunity to leverage other gifts.

When presented with a proposed challenge gift or seeking to solicit one, Smith suggests that organizations begin by talking with the donor about what it is he or she expects the challenge to accomplish for the organization.

She says that including the donor in discussions about what the donor would like to see happen and the degree to which that is realistic and may be accomplished is important. "Is the donor envisioning that the challenge will spur gifts to the organization from people who have never given before? Does the donor wish to challenge a specific constituency (e.g., doctors in the region, alumni from 1962, current/past board members and other organization volunteers)? Does the donor hope the challenge will encourage increased gifts from those who regularly give?"

Other points to negotiate with the donor, Smith says:

✓ **Time to fulfill challenge.** Short-term challenges create a sense of urgency; if an organization has capacity and ability to bring in lots of gifts quickly, that might be a good way to go, she says: "I worked with a foundation that received a $500,000 challenge and was given 90 days to match it dollar-for-dollar. They did it, though it was a bit of a stretch. Challenges are good for those kinds of realistic stretches. Too long a time period to fulfill the challenge may not be best — the urgency is lost and potential donors forget about it.... A challenge that lasts more than six to 12 months may not be as effective as one that lasts three to four months."

✓ **The match ratio.** Challenges can be 1:1 (challenge matches donations dollar for dollar), 2:1 (challenge donor doubles each gift made by donor), 3:1, or even 4:1, she says. Or they can set a specific dollar goal. For example, if the organization can raise a specified percentage more than it typically does annually, or a specific dollar amount greater than what is usually raised, the donor will make his/her gift.

Be specific about what you are asking potential donors to do, says Smith. "Challenges are best when potential givers understand that the fate of the challenge gift depends on their acting. A challenge that says 'You'll get this no matter what, just do your best' isn't really the same kind of challenge as one that says, 'In order to get my six-figure gift in full, you have to meet all the time conditions and dollar goals we agreed to and if you do not, the challenge goes away.' The urgency is what drives it."

Source: Susan D. Smith, Consultant, Susan D. Smith Consultant in Philanthropy, Barneveld, NY. Phone (315) 896-8524. E-mail: sdsmith@ntcnet.com

Focus on Improving Quality of Grant Proposals

 What have you found to be the most effective ways to respond to a request for an increase in your grant proposal production rate?

"If I were asked to meet a fixed goal, I would probably respond:

'How would you like me to approach the fundraising process? If my solicitations are to be the cold-call type, with no prior donor cultivation, I can achieve a high proposal rate, but with a low success rate in terms of securing gifts. If I'm to cultivate the donor first, my proposal rate won't be as high, but we'll enjoy a much better success rate. Cultivating before soliciting is like priming before painting. You can paint without priming, but your paint job won't look as good and it won't last as long. So please define what you want me to achieve: a high proposal rate or a high success rate.'"

— *Dennis Alexander, Director of Foundation Relations, Texas Christian University (Fort Worth, TX)*

"We'll all face these demands during the coming months because of falling endowment values, expanding fiscal needs along with contracting wallets and greater competition for corporate and foundation dollars. But we won't get more dollars by sending out more proposals, but rather by sending out better, more compelling ones. That means designing better projects and presenting them effectively. Those two things don't happen well under pressure. So I would say: 'I can certainly write more proposals every month, but I'm assuming that what you really want is a greater number of positive responses. In order to represent this institution positively and get positive responses, I need to target my proposals carefully, to collaborate appropriately, to communicate carefully, and to produce the best request we can. Each of those takes time — and if you're pushing me for more proposals, those are the things I will have to sacrifice in order to meet your goal.'"

— *Nancy J. Doemel, Senior Advancement Officer and Coordinator of Volunteer Services, Wabash College (Crawfordsville, IN)*

Four-star Assessment Boosts College's Efforts

Calvin College (Grand Rapids, MI) recently received a special honor from the independent charity evaluator, Charity Navigator (Mahwah, NJ): four stars.

That's Charity Navigator's highest ranking for a 501(c)(3) organization — a big deal to be sure, but Phil de Haan, Calvin's director of communications and marketing, says the ranking is really just a bonus, not the reason they do what they do.

"We've never run our fundraising operation at Calvin with an eye toward the rankings. We've always felt that our fundraising operation at Calvin College is effective and efficient," de Haan says.

Supporting that belief is the fact that organizers of Calvin's most recent capital campaign actually beat their $150 million goal by $5 million.

How did Calvin garner the top ranking from Charity Navigator?

"There was not a lot that Calvin had to do," de Haan says. "Charity Navigator does all of the legwork in terms of finding the data they need to make an informed and complete evaluation. On our end our main responsibility was simply doing things right — filing IRS Form 990 and working hard to be responsible and trustworthy stewards of the financial resources people entrust to us."

That work includes helping people understand why supporting the college is important and that Calvin officials will be good stewards of those gifts, de Haan says, adding: "Something like the Charity Navigator ranking is one more thing that gives people confidence in Calvin."

Source: Phil de Haan, Director, Communications and Marketing, Calvin College, Grand Rapids, MI. Phone (616) 526-6000. E-mail: dehp@calvin.edu

Ripple Effect Waves in Support for Capital Campaign

Phil de Haan, director of communications and marketing, Calvin College (Grand Rapids, MI), says ongoing efforts to develop meaningful and lasting relationships with donors were critical in the success of their recent $155 million capital campaign.

One tool that helped build loyalty with prospective donors was telling stories of alumni impacting the world and thus living out the mission of the college, which in part states that Calvin students "offer their hearts and lives to do God's work in God's world."

In sharing the stories, de Haan says they were able to say that a gift to Calvin was not just helping the college and its students, but many other projects and organizations worldwide. That ripple-effect argument was a positive message during the campaign that resonated with donors and helped contribute to the campaign's overwhelming success.

Could Charity Navigator Give Your Fundraising a Boost?

Could your organization benefit from an evaluation by Charity Navigator (Mahwah, NJ)?

Founded in 2001, Charity Navigator offers an objective, numbers-based rating system to assess the financial health of more than 5,000 of America's best-known charities. Named as one of Time magazine's 50 coolest websites, www.charitynavigator.com — the website for Charity Navigator — helps guide philanthropic giving and, in its own words, helps nonprofits "by shining lights on truly effective organizations."

The company considers these guidelines before evaluating any organization:

1. **Tax status.** Charities must have tax-exempt status under Section 501(c)(3) of the Internal Revenue Service Code and file Form 990.

2. **Source of revenue.** Public support must be $500,000-plus in most recent fiscal year.

3. **Length of operation.** Organizations must have filed four years of 990 forms to be considered.

4. **Location.** Scope of nonprofit's work can be international, but operations must be located in the United States and organization must be registered with the IRS.

5. **Program types.** According to its website, Charity Navigator is not currently accepting hospitals, hospital foundations, universities, community foundations, PBS stations, land trusts or preserves.

To have your organization evaluated by Charity Navigator, register at www.charitynavigator.org and complete the online request form. Registering gives access to advanced benchmarking tools.

Help Your Employees Pursue Grants

At Connecticut College (New London, CT), staff in the corporate, foundation and government relations office created a website section to help faculty learn more about grants and how to pursue them.

The corporate, foundation and government relations staff works with faculty on research and travel grants, and drafts proposals for institutional projects and priorities. It also serves as a link to hundreds of public and private organizations that support the college's mission.

Resources on the college website (www.conncoll.edu/giving/2059.htm) include:

✓ **Sponsored research links** such as a fellowships calendar, registration for the National Science Foundation's Fastlane site and websites for researching grant opportunities.

✓ **Grant information** to help with the application process, such as grant proposal guidelines, tips on proposal writing and a glossary of terms.

✓ **Forms** such as a checklist for submitting a proposal, a funding research assistance form, a grant application approval form, and an approval process flow chart.

✓ **Policies and Procedures** such as accounting policies, post-award procedures, responsible conduct of research policy, and intellectual property and technology transfer policy.

✓ **Recent grant awards** to Connecticut College faculty.

College faculty find the site very helpful, says Kristin Geshel, faculty grants and government relations officer. "It gives them a good start at finding funding opportunities."

The key is getting people to look at the website, she says. She shows current faculty the website and does a presentation that includes an introduction of the website to all new faculty. She also provides a link to the website in her e-mail signature.

"Having these resources available to faculty on the website has helped me greatly," says Geshel. "It has created a team approach to grant writing. Faculty expertise in their research plus my experience at finding funding opportunities increases the chances of finding a good fit for their needs."

Making the website accessible to the public shows external funders that they have a team approach to seeking grants, she says. "Nothing on the site is confidential or proprietary, so there's no reason not to make the site public," says Geshel. "Also, posting the awards allows faculty to see what their colleagues are doing and increases their interest in grant writing."

Source: Kristin Geshel, Faculty Grants and Government Relations Officer, Connecticut College, New London, CT. Phone (860) 439-2438. E-mail: Kristin.geshel@conncoll.edu

---

Make the Most Of a Corporate Gift

About to receive a corporate gift? Before popping the final question, consider including this caveat:

"Would it be possible to set up your corporate gift as a challenge that will match all of your employees', board members' and vendors' gifts to our campaign?"

Useful References for Grant Seekers

Here's a sampling of links and resources you can turn to for additional help in seeking foundation and corporate grants:

American Association of Grant Professionals — http://grantprofessionals.org/ — a nonprofit membership association that works to build and support an international community of grant professionals.

American Grant Writers' Association — http://www.agwa.us/ — association's mission is "to enhance the community of grantseekers' professional standards and ethical practices through education, certification, networking and professional growth."

Fundsnet Services ONLINE — http://www.fundsnetservices.com/ — offers resource assistance to those in need of funding for their programs and initiatives.

Grants.gov — http://www.grants.gov/ — source to find and apply for federal grants.

National Science Foundation — http://www.nsf.gov/index.jsp — independent federal agency created "to promote the progress of science; to advance the national health, prosperity, and welfare; to secure the national defense..."

The Foundation Center — http://foundationcenter.org/ — recognized as the nation's leading authority on organized philanthropy, connecting nonprofits and the grantmakers supporting them to tools they can use and information they can trust.

The Grantsmanship Center — http://www.tgci.com/ — offers grantsmanship training to nonprofit and government agencies.